The Revolutionary, Science-Based
Alcoholism and Addiction Recovery Program

Healing the Addicted Brain

HAROLD C. URSCHEL, III, MD

CEO and Founder of the Urschel Recovery Science Institute and www.EnterHealth.com

sourcebooks

Published by Sourcebooks, Inc.
P.O. Box 4410, Naperville, Illinois 60567-4410
(630) 961-3900
Fax: (630) 961-2168
www.sourcebooks.com

Library of Congress Cataloging-in-Publication Data
Urschel, Harold.
  Healing the addicted brain : the revolutionary, science-based alcoholism and addiction recovery program / Harold Urschel.
      p. cm.
  Includes index.
  1. Alcoholism—Treatment. 2. Substance abuse—Treatment. 3. Brain—Effect of drugs on. I. Title.
  RC565.U77 2009
  616.86'06—dc22
                          2008045016

Printed and bound in the United States of America.
BG 25 24 23 22 21

To my wife, Christi, and two sons, Chance and Carr, for encouraging me to write a book that would really make a difference.

CONTENTS

Introduction

Addiction is a lifelong disease, and to many who are caught in its web, it can seem like finding the right treatment takes just about as long.

If you're struggling with addiction, there's a good chance you've already seen several physicians and psychologists, have been through an inpatient or outpatient ("at home") treatment program, and have had exhaustive rounds of "talking therapy," which you were told was the state-of-the-art approach to curing addiction. Despite all this treatment, you are still addicted. Your work performance is suffering and family relations fraying; you either have screaming fights with your spouse/significant other or have retreated into a sullen, secretive silence. You're still spending much too much money on your habit, and your children are still at risk of physical and emotional damage.

If you're a member of an addict's family, or perhaps a close sober friend, you feel as if you've heard too many failed promises to sober up, covered up too much bad behavior, watched the family be pulled apart and the finances drained, and stood by helplessly as dreams were shattered and the life of the addict slowly slipped away. You've been through the emotional wringer too many times and seen the latest "guaranteed treatment" fail repeatedly. Sometimes you wish you could just walk away from it all—but you know you can't and feel absolutely stuck.

Through it all, whether you're the addict or the family member, you've wondered if there is any point to treatment. Why have your hopes been dashed over and over again? Why not just accept the obvious fact that an addict is an addict, and addiction is ultimately untreatable?

Before they came to me for help, many of my patients and their families feel that way, with good reason. Traditionally, the success rate for addiction treatment was abysmally low. A few of the medicines we had available were effective, but their use was limited or restricted for various reasons. The treatment most health experts pinned their hopes on, talking therapy, was not very successful. As a result, most addicts, their families, and friends were repeatedly disappointed. Understandably, many simply gave up.

I'm here to tell you that you no longer have to feel helpless and hopeless. There *is* hope, new hope that stems from a new scientific understanding of the nature of addiction plus novel medicines that finally allow us to control cravings and fix the physical damage to the brain caused by addiction. We now know that addiction is a chronic brain disease, that brain damage interferes with the addict's ability to respond to talking therapy, and that once the physical brain damage has been repaired, talking therapy and other elements of traditional treatment can be very successful.

We're at the beginning of a new era in addiction medicine, armed with a fresh view of the disease plus high-tech medicines and other treatments that will allow success for up to 90 percent of those who seek help. This is not just a tremendous improvement in the treatment rate; it represents a paradigm shift that will help us to turn the understanding of addiction from a shameful habit that destroys lives into a treatable illness.

I know you may have been disappointed before, but I can tell you that there is good reason for hope. The ideas and treatment concepts described in this book can help you regain your life or that of your loved one.

This book offers a comprehensive look at the new understanding of addiction and its treatment. Reading through it will arm you with the latest treatment information and ideas to help you to get the most from your recovery program—or help a loved one through treatment. However, space limitations prevented me from providing the many checklists, inventories, worksheets, and even some ideas that I normally make available to my patients. If you would like to see these documents, and learn even more about the latest addiction treatments, look for this symbol throughout the text: ●. This indicates that there are checklists, inventories, or worksheets, or perhaps additional information, to be found at www. EnterHealth.com/HealingtheAddictedBrain, a state-of-the-art website I developed to provide education and support for alcoholics, addicts, and their families.

The "secret sauce" in this book is science. Through this book, the EnterHealth.com website, the Urschel Recovery Science Institute, and my lectures, I continually strive to introduce the latest scientific research findings into everyday clinical practice. The National Institutes of Health spend hundreds of millions of dollars a year looking for new methods and medications to treat addiction. Unfortunately, the findings from this research rarely make their way into clinical addiction treatment programs. My goal is to change that, immediately and forever. The latest and best research findings on heart disease, diabetes, and other chronic diseases are regularly and rapidly translated into improved clinical practice; it's time for that to happen in addiction treatment as well.

It's because of my emphasis on the science of addiction treatment that I call my concepts Recovery Science. As I take you through each of the major topics you need to understand and apply to your own or a loved one's recovery program, I will interject the latest scientific research into my discussions.

I want to finish this introduction with an important warning. Although you will get the latest information on understanding and treating addiction in this book, it is specifically designed to be used in concert with a real-life treatment program, or the education and support that you will find on www.EnterHealth.com/HealingtheAddictedBrain. You can no more cure addiction with this book alone than you can treat diabetes successfully just by reading a book on that disease. Medicine is a science, but it is also an art that requires applying a variety of important "rules" to different people with different individual needs. You will learn the overarching treatment concepts and topics in this book, but each person is unique and must be guided by a healthcare provider, therapist/coach, and sponsor who can create a successful addiction recovery program. Learn from this book, share it with your family, sponsor, and healthcare provider, but allow them to help you beat this life-threatening illness. If you do this, your chances of recovery approach 90 percent—an amazing number for any chronic illness.

I won't say it will be easy for you to maintain sobriety, but following the Recovery Science principles and recommendations, it is *doable!*

CHAPTER ONE

It's a Disease!

Everything you know about addiction treatment is wrong.

I can safely make this statement to most laypeople—plus an alarmingly large number of health professionals—without fear of being contradicted. Why? Because most people know very little about addiction, and what they *do* know (or think they know) boils down to this: addicts can quit if they really want to; all they have to do is commit wholeheartedly to their treatment, which consists largely of "talking therapy"—individual or group psychotherapy or 12-step programs like Alcoholics Anonymous.

That's the sum total of most people's knowledge of addiction treatment. But it's dead wrong. And it's the main reason that the success rate for addiction treatment is currently only 20–30 percent. This means that 70–80 percent of the participants in any given addiction treatment program will *not* be successful. No wonder people think that alcohol or drug addiction treatment doesn't work!

Fortunately, recent scientific research has discovered new avenues of treatment by showing conclusively that addiction is *a chronic physical disease* that attacks the brain, damaging key parts of the cerebral cortex

and limbic system. This brain damage cannot be reversed by talking therapies; only select new medications and continued sobriety can do that.
But when used together, these new medicines and talking therapies can
literally work wonders.

In this chapter we'll look at the new scientific research on addiction
and its effects on the brain. (Throughout the book I'll use the word "addict" to refer to both alcoholics and drug addicts, and "addiction" to
refer to both alcohol and drug addiction, unless otherwise specified.)
You'll learn what happens inside the brain of a person with an addiction,
why talking therapy alone doesn't usually work, and how medications
can help the brain repair itself, pushing the treatment success rate up as
high as 90 percent!

Myths That Lead to Unsuccessful Treatment of Addiction

Addiction is a serious brain disease that has reached epidemic proportions
in the United States. The shocking statistics say it all:

- According to the 2006 National Survey on Drug Use and Health,
  about 22.6 million Americans aged twelve or older abused or were
  dependent on a substance during the previous year (9.2 percent of
  the population aged twelve or older).

- Of these, 15.6 million abused or were dependent on alcohol but not
  illegal drugs.

- 3.8 million abused or were dependent on illegal drugs but
  not alcohol.

- 3.2 million abused or were dependent on *both* alcohol and
  illegal drugs.

- Approximately 9–10 percent of children ages twelve to seventeen use
  illegal drugs, and about the same percentage report binge drinking.

- Each year, well over two million adults use pain relievers for non-
  medical reasons.

- Over ten million full-time workers between the ages of eighteen and sixty-four abuse or are dependent on alcohol.
- There are roughly one million drug-related visits to U.S. emergency rooms every year.
- Americans spend close to $20 billion a year on treatment for alcohol and drug problems.
- Seventy-five percent of alcoholics never enter a treatment program.
- Of those who do seek treatment for addiction, 70–80 percent suffer a relapse soon after "graduating" from these programs.

But perhaps the most frightening statistic of all is the death toll. *Alcoholism is the third leading cause of death in the United States, right on the heels of heart disease and cancer.* And although no one knows exactly how many additional lives are lost to the abuse of and addiction to drugs, the figure is surely in the tens of thousands per year.

Forty-five-year-old Simon, a high-level chemist at a Dallas-based manufacturer, was referred to me by a drug court judge when he was charged with his second DWI and facing a ten-year prison sentence. His life was in shambles. Alcoholism had put Simon's career in jeopardy and played a major part in the dissolution of his twenty-five-year marriage three years earlier. Since that time, Simon's drinking had progressed significantly. Of his three children, only his son was still speaking to him. Both of his daughters had banned him from their homes after he repeatedly showed up intoxicated and frightened their children. And alcoholism was beginning to take a toll on his health. His blood pressure and cholesterol levels were dangerously high, two classic signs of heart disease. And the whites of his eyes had taken on a yellowish tinge, indicating malfunction of the liver. All of these problems, his doctor told him, were directly related to his alcohol use. And yet he had never sought or received any treatment for his alcoholism.

Simon's story is not unusual. A full 75 percent of alcoholics are *not* in treatment for an illness that causes nearly as many deaths as heart disease or cancer. Why isn't our current treatment system working? At the inception, our ability to prevent and treat addiction is drastically hampered by two myths.

- Myth #1: *Addiction is a kind of "personality disease."* People with addictions are often branded losers, sinners who refuse to face up to their evil ways, or weaklings who can't "suck it up" long enough to throw off their bad habits. The media does much to contribute to this belief. We've all seen the endless parade of stories about Lindsay Lohan, Robert Downey, Jr., Charlie Sheen, and countless other celebrities who bounce in and out of treatment programs. But after spending $80,000–$100,000 a month for treatment, they all seem to race right out to a bar or to meet their dealers, diving head first back into old destructive behaviors. Since they appear to be getting the best possible (or at least most expensive) treatment available, the perception is that it must be their own fault that they can't stay sober; they must not be trying hard enough.

- Myth #2: *"Talking therapy" is the only significant treatment.* Talking therapy is a series of discussions through which the addicted person learns the coping skills needed to deal effectively with stress and other issues related to the addiction. Most health professionals—physicians, psychiatrists, psychologists, and addiction counselors alike—believe that the best possible treatment for alcohol or drug addiction is some sort of talking therapy, such as group therapy plus individual counseling, coupled with participation in an ongoing 12-step program. Unfortunately, this approach works for only a meager 30 percent of patients, a fact that has convinced most healthcare providers that addiction is not treatable.

For decades these two fallacies have put a stranglehold on the development of effective new therapies for addiction. They've robbed addicted people and their families of hope and have cost our country millions of lives and hundreds of billions of dollars.

Jason, a fifty-five-year-old welder, tried to get help for his alcoholism after he went through his third divorce. At the time, he was putting away about a quart of vodka a day and knew it was seriously affecting his work and his personal life. So one day at lunchtime, Jason showed up at an AA meeting around the corner from where he was working. But within ten minutes he had categorized those at the meeting as a bunch of hopeless loser alcoholics who were nothing like him. Jason assured himself that he could give up alcohol on his own; he didn't need any help. But after just one alcohol-free evening, Jason awoke to trembling hands and legs and a strong urge to drink. He decided that it would be okay to have just one small drink to steady his nerves. Naturally, this was only the beginning, and his "quart a day" habit was quickly reinstated. About six months later, after being charged with his first DWI, Jason checked himself into rehab for a weeklong inpatient detoxification. When he left rehab, he was supposed to attend classes on alcohol education and go to AA meetings regularly. But just six days after he went home, Jason started drinking again.

What's wrong with our current ways of treating addiction? Why do they fail so often and so miserably? Obviously, we need to take an entirely new approach. We need a paradigm shift, a new approach that will do for the treatment of addiction what insulin did for diabetes, what Prozac did for depression, and what Viagra did for erectile dysfunction.

Fortunately, science has recently provided some brand-new insights into addiction. Now we can definitively say that it is a chronic medical illness, a disease of the brain that *can and must* be treated like other chronic medical illnesses—such as diabetes, hypertension, or asthma—that alter the physiological workings of the body.

Birth of an Addiction

Many patients ask me why this is happening to them. "Everybody I know drinks," they'll say. "How come they can drink a little and stop, but I can't?" Others note that their friends smoke some marijuana or snort a few lines once in a while but "keep it under control," while they become full-fledged addicts.

We can't say exactly why you became addicted to alcohol or drugs, but we do know that there are certain risk factors making one person more susceptible to addiction than another. These include:

- *Genetics*—Certain genetic factors may increase your vulnerability to addiction, making you "more susceptible" to developing the disease more easily. In other words, a family history of addiction makes you more likely to develop it yourself.

- *Emotional state*—High levels of stress, anxiety, or emotional pain can lead some people to use alcohol or drugs in an attempt to "block out" the turmoil. The levels and persistence of certain stress hormones may be associated with an easier slide into addiction.

- *Psychological factors*—Suffering from depression or low self-esteem makes you three times more likely to use alcohol or drugs excessively and become addicted. Adults with inadequately treated attention deficit/hyperactivity disorder also may be more likely to become dependent on alcohol or drugs.

- *Social and cultural factors*—Having friends or a close partner who drinks or uses regularly—even if not to the point of addiction—could promote excessive drinking or use on your part. It may be difficult for you to distance yourself from these "enablers," or at least from their drinking/using habits. In addition, the glamorous way that drinking alcohol is portrayed in advertising and in the media may send the message that it's okay to drink excessively.

- *Age*—People who begin drinking or using drugs at an early age, by age sixteen or earlier, are 40 percent more likely to become addicted than people who wait to use alcohol or drugs until they're 21 years old. That's right—you have a 40 percent lower chance of becoming addicted if you wait to use alcohol or drugs until you're 21.

• *Gender*—Men are more likely to become dependent on or abuse alcohol than are women.

These factors offer rough guidelines as to who is more likely to become addicted, and may help to explain why you or a loved one became an addict.

How Alcohol Harms the Brain

In the not-too-distant past, it was necessary to wait until an addict died before physically inspecting his or her brain, before weighing, measuring, and looking for damaged areas. This information was helpful but limited, for there's only so much to be learned from a dead brain.

Today, high-tech tools—including MRI, fMRI (functional magnetic resonance imaging), DTI (diffusion tensor imaging), SPECT and PET (positron emission tomography)—allow us to see the brain in unprecedented

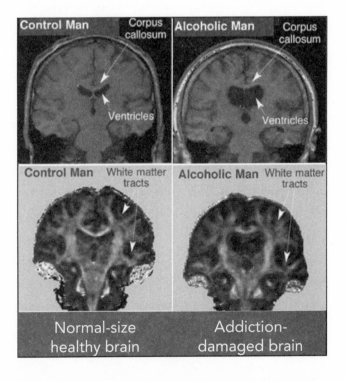

new detail while it is alive and functioning. We can literally watch the brain in action, measure its ability to function, and track both damage and repair as they occur.

Because of these scientific advances, in just a few years we have learned a great deal about how the excessive ingestion of alcohol or drugs damages the brain over time. Perhaps the most obvious damage is shrinkage caused by the destruction of brain cells. Months, years, or decades of excessive alcohol or drug consumption cause a healthy, normal-sized brain to shrivel. Thus, alcoholics/heavy drinkers literally have less brain matter to work with. This is a fact that has been documented many times.

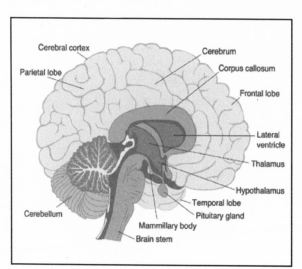

Much of the shrinkage of the brain occurs in the cortex of the brain's frontal lobe. The cortex is the outer layer of the brain, a heavily folded area full of canyon-like grooves that wraps around and over the brain. The frontal lobe, which is located just behind the forehead, plays an important role in decision making, judgment, impulse control, problem solving, and other intellectual skills, and also influences the regulation of social and sexual behavior. Damage to this area of the brain makes it difficult, if not impossible, for the addict to understand why getting "blitzed" all the time is so dangerous and why it's important to pay attention to things like work, family, and health. Not surprisingly, the damaged brain can find it nearly impossible to focus on recovery from the addiction.

The frontal lobe is not the only part of the brain that alcohol damages. The cerebellum and other parts of the cortex also shrivel when awash in alcohol. Together, these parts of the brain help regulate thinking, reasoning, planning, organizing, balance, coordination, walking, running, dancing, and all other kinds of movement.

Altering the Brain's Communication System

Alcoholism also harms the brain in more subtle ways that disrupt the brain's communication system.

Essentially, the brain is a communication, data interpretation, and storage device. Brain cells receive data from inside the body (for example, the skin temperature of the big toe, the fullness or emptiness of the stomach) and from outside the body (for example, what the boss is saying, the color and size of the clouds in the sky). This information is analyzed and interpreted by certain brain cells, which send action instructions to other brain cells, which forward these orders to the body. All of the incoming and outgoing information is communicated by and stored within appropriate brain cells.

In order for this complex system to work, the billions of brain cells in your head must be able to "talk" to each other instantly and easily. They do so via long rods (called axons and dendrites) that extend from the center of a nerve cell. The rods don't actually touch each other; instead, the end of one comes right up to the end of another, leaving a tiny gap between the two. When Cell #1 wants to "say something" to Cell #2, it secretes a specific communication chemical called a neurotransmitter that travels from one rod to another. Which neurotransmitter is chosen will depend upon what Cell #1 wants to communicate.

Sliding across the gap between the rods, the neurotransmitter will slip into a little area called a receptor on Cell #2's rod, but not just any receptor. It only fits into a certain kind of receptor, just as a key only fits a certain lock. Once the neurotransmitter settles into the receptor, it triggers a flash of recognition in Cell #2; the presence of that specific communication chemical in that particular receptor tells this cell exactly what it is supposed to do in response. Depending on Cell #2's job in the brain, the response might be to order the heart to beat faster, the mouth to deliver an apology, the left hand to swat a mosquito, and so on.

This explanation may seem simple, but the brain's communication system is very complex. In order for it to work properly, the right kinds and amounts of chemical messengers must be secreted by the "talking cells" at exactly the right times. There must also be just the right number and right kinds of receptors on the receiving cells. Think of what might, in a very simplified sense, go wrong:

- If the "speaking cell" doesn't have enough of the necessary neurotransmitters, it will only be able to "whisper" its message, or perhaps it will become completely mute.

- If the "speaking cell" has *too much* of a certain kind of neurotransmitter, it may be encouraged to say things it doesn't mean.

- If the "listening cell" doesn't have enough of the necessary receptors, it won't be able to hear the message, or will hear it only faintly.

- If the "listening cell" has *too many* of a certain kind of receptor, it can listen desperately for one particular message, perhaps ignoring others.

Suppose every time your good friend tried to say, "Set the drink down, and go home," his voice became a barely audible whisper. Or what if your ears could only hear people shouting, "Party! Party!" and nothing else? That's what it's like in your brain when your neurotransmitter system isn't working properly.

Chronic alcohol ingestion is thought to injure the complex, yet fragile, brain communication systems and can throw a monkey wrench in the brain's internal communications by altering the amounts, types, and ratios of neurotransmitters, as well as the numbers, kinds, and ratios of neurotransmitter receptor sites. For example, chronic consumption of alcohol causes the release of overly abundant amounts of the neurotransmitters serotonin and dopamine. These two "pleasure" messengers contribute to the feeling of being high—and make you want to get high again. Having large amounts of serotonin and dopamine in your brain's circulation is like having millions of little people in your brain, all of whom are drinking, having a good time, and offering you a beer.

This injury from excessive alcohol ingestion can also work the opposite way, causing brain cells to "close down" receptors for a messenger called GABA (gamma-aminobutyric acid). GABA inhibits agitation and helps to keep you calm. With too little GABA, even when the thought "I've had enough" does enter your brain, it may not be heard well, because there aren't enough "ears" listening for it.

Alcohol also increases the number of glutamine receptor sites, which, among other things, play a role in seizures. If they aren't kept "full" of alcohol-driven chemical messengers, they can rev up your entire system and may even trigger seizures. We know of at least forty other major neurotransmitter systems in the brain, all of which are disrupted by chronic alcohol use.

These and other brain changes make it incredibly difficult for the alcoholic to ignore the "bad" messages and hear the "good" ones. Can you imagine how difficult it is to achieve and maintain sobriety with a shrunken brain that's hammered with messages like, "Gotta feel good, gotta drink!" all day long? When any thought of giving up drinking comes across as a whisper? When the brain is full of activating/stimulating signals that, if not satisfied by the presence of sufficient alcohol, may trigger a seizure?

What happens when you stop drinking? Suddenly, the substance that both damaged your brain and flooded it with harmful messages disappears. But everything is *not* all right—far from it. Your brain does *not* right itself overnight; it does not eliminate the extra "get drunk!" messages and remove the excess "love to party!" receptors. It does *not* immediately manufacture additional "pay close attention to your counselor while sipping tea" messages, or construct new "being calm is pleasant" receptors. In an alcoholic's injured disease state, the brain—down to the last cell—still desperately wants its alcohol. It does *not* want to change; it likes things exactly the way they are. *That's why addiction is considered a disease. It's not a character flaw or moral failing, not a result of laziness or selfishness, but a long-term illness caused by measurable physical damage to the brain.*

And that's why most addicts can't just give up their drug of choice, follow a carefully reasoned argument explaining why it's better to be sober, stop thinking about getting high, or stop blowing the family's money on drugs. *They can't do these things because the disease has damaged their brains,* just as the disease of hypertension damages the arteries and the disease of diabetes damages the kidneys. You wouldn't put your face to the belly of a diabetic and shout, "Hey, you kidneys in there! Quit slacking off! Start processing the urine properly, right now!" The diabetes-damaged kidneys are not capable of hearing or responding to your command. Neither is the damaged brain of the alcoholic or addict.

Luckily, the "I've got to have it!" messages fade with time, and the brain does repair itself (a fact that scientists have only recently discovered). This is true even in older people. But at any age, it takes a long time (with alcohol usually at least four to twelve months) to restore the brain even closer to its original, sober healthy form—and in many cases, it doesn't completely return to its original, pre-addiction state.

A Graphic Look at the Brain Damage

Another way to understand how alcohol damages the brain is to track the use of glucose, the "brain fuel." Brain cells use glucose exclusively for the energy they need to function. By measuring the amount of glucose used by cells in various areas of the brain, scientists can tell which cells are working properly and which ones have been impaired by alcohol or drug use.

Damage, in the form of changes in the kinds and amounts of neurotransmitters and receptors, alterations in glucose usage, and other differences, occurs in many areas of the brain, including the following:

- *Cortex*—the outer area of the brain, which contains the most highly evolved cells, where abstract thinking, decision making, and higher cognitive processes occur, allowing us to think, learn, and understand.

- *Limbic region*—a structure deep inside the brain that controls desires and the body's basic drives. Powerful behaviors such as eating, drinking, and sexual behavior are housed in this area, which is filled with intertwining emotional circuits that give these drives irresistible emotional power, because the brain's pleasure center (dopamine) is housed here.

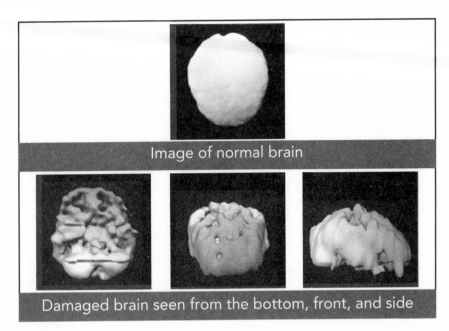

Image of normal brain

Damaged brain seen from the bottom, front, and side

- *Hippocampus*—an area adjacent to the limbic region where many long-term memory cells reside, all of which are "plugged in" to the limbic region's emotional circuits.

The upshot is a damaged brain that's programmed to do the wrong thing, over and over again.

The pictures above show some of the physical damage to the brain that's caused by excessive alcohol consumption. The top image, which comes from an imaging test called a SPECT, shows a normal brain. The other three images are views of the brain of a thirty-eight-year-old who drank heavily on weekends for seventeen years. The images of the alcohol-damaged brain show obvious physical injury, plus a marked decrease in overall activity. In nontechnical terms, the damaged brain looks like a big chunk of polar ice that's half-melted and full of crevices.

These images say it all. Alcohol and addictive drugs physically damage and transform the brain, in the same way that other chronic diseases damage other parts of the body.

Addiction Is a Chronic Medical Illness

We're accustomed to having our ailments alleviated. Infections are typically cured with antibiotics in a few days, while broken bones are usually healed in a few weeks. Even failing kidneys and damaged joints can be replaced, restoring pain-free movement and function in a few weeks or months.

Thanks largely to our latest, excellent medicines and surgical procedures, many of our current ailments and diseases are acute, which means they come on fast, rise to a peak, and then vanish rapidly. You notice a throbbing pain in your forehead at 11:00 a.m., take an aspirin, and before you sit down to lunch, the pain is gone. You cut your hand and develop an infection on Monday, by Wednesday you're at the doctor's office receiving a prescription for antibiotics, and by Friday the problem is resolved.

Unfortunately, addiction-related brain damage is not a "quick come, quick go" disease. It takes quite a while for the brain damage to become evident and an agonizingly long time to repair it. And from the early stages of brain damage through to the very end of the long repair process, the addict is caught in the clutches of a very powerful, life-threatening illness. Even after the brain has been fully repaired—*if* it is ever fully repaired—the addict may still be at greater-than-average risk of sliding back into drinking or using again, thanks to the factors that encouraged the addiction in the first place.

Arthur, a twenty-seven-year-old musician addicted to alcohol, heroin, and cocaine, had been in four different residential treatment programs during the previous five years. Still, his longest period of sobriety was only thirty days. As a result of his use, Arthur had been in multiple accidents resulting in a significant amount of pain, the most recent being a motorcycle accident that fractured his neck. He treated a great deal of his pain with alcohol and recreational drugs and also used these substances to calm his ADHD. Arthur had tried AA and NA in the past but couldn't seem to stick with the program. His loved ones were exasperated and no longer interested in paying for treatment. After all, what was the point? Treatment just didn't work.

Like diabetes, asthma, and other chronic diseases, addiction is a lifelong illness. Your diabetes is not cured simply because you're taking your medicine and watching your diet; it may be controlled, but it's still present. It's the same with the disease of addiction; it can be controlled but never completely eliminated.

The length of the repair process depends on many factors, including the substances that were abused, the length of use, the extent of the abuse, and the individual's genetic and biochemical makeup. As a general rule, it takes at least four to twelve months of complete sobriety before significant brain repair is achieved.

There are no quick fixes for the disease of addiction, which is why addicts deserve sympathy and support, even when they lapse. We don't condemn a diabetic for having a sugary dessert or forgetting to take his or her medicine; we don't revile the person with hypertension who gains weight instead of losing it. Instead, we sympathize with and understand the inner urges that caused them to "oops," and we encourage them to take their medicines regularly and stick to a health-enhancing eating and exercise plan. We are understanding, in spite of the fact that people with critical diseases such as diabetes, asthma, and elevated blood pressure often *do* neglect to follow their doctors' orders. Less than 50 percent of patients with these diseases take their medicines as prescribed, and less than 30 percent comply with lifestyle changes recommended by their doctors. The relapse rates for these three illnesses—measured by the number of people who have to go to emergency rooms, the hospital, or their doctors' offices on an emergency basis—is 40–60 percent a year. And these frightening statistics are for people who do *not* have a chronic brain disease. Think how difficult it must be for those who do have addiction-addled brains to follow their doctors' orders! Why should we treat addicts differently, and so much more harshly, than we do other people with chronic illnesses?

Is Anyone Listening?

Unfortunately, we *do* treat addicts differently. We beg, plead, nag, and try to bully them into improving their ways, which is about as helpful as ordering a diabetic kidney to work better.

For the past several decades, the primary treatment for addicts in various types of inpatient and outpatient programs has been a combination of detoxification, some form of "talking therapy," such as cognitive behavioral psychotherapy, and 12-step referrals.

Talking therapy is designed to influence the cells in the higher cognitive centers of the cortex. It can and does work, but *only* if the brain is willing and able to pay attention, listen, and remember. Yet most addicted brains are physically incapable of generating the focus and cooperation necessary for this type of therapy to work. Until the damage has been at least partially repaired, most brains are in no condition to absorb and digest these new ideas. So when a person goes to treatment (inpatient or outpatient talking therapy) during their first ninety days of sobriety, their therapist/sponsor is giving them critical, life-saving information during the time their injured brain can least absorb and remember it. No wonder relapse is so common during the first three to four months.

A great deal of the alcohol- or drug-induced brain damage takes place in the prefrontal cortex—where planning, abstract thinking, and the regulation

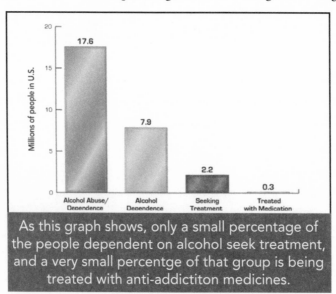

As this graph shows, only a small percentage of the people dependent on alcohol seek treatment, and a very small percentge of that group is being treated with anti-addictiton medicines.

of impulse behavior, drives, and compulsive repetitive behaviors occur—and in the limbic region, an area deep inside the brain that is responsible for powerful, primal drives such as hunger, thirst, the need to bond, and the need for sexual contact. Talking therapy can help correct problems in the cortex, but it cannot directly influence the limbic system or other structures found deeper within the brain. This means that until recently there's been no way to reach the limbic system or these other brain injured structures that deal with emotions and very powerful specific memories. Yet these parts of the brain have created deep emotional connections between using and pleasure that the brain "remembers" very well. This means that even

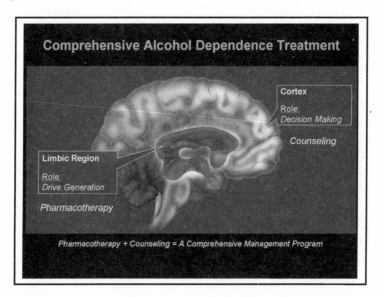

if the addict is able to listen to and understand the therapy, that nearly irresistible emotional drive to get high will remain intact. No matter how much an addict might "get" the don't-get-high argument, it continues to be very difficult to "just say no" to these powerful, primal urges—as difficult to resist, in fact, as the urge to drink filthy, polluted water after wandering through the desert for several days without a drink, or the urge to turn to cannibalism after being stranded on a deserted island with no other food.

That's why so many addicts relapse early in the recovery process; they simply cannot "get" what their well-intentioned counselors want them to understand. And even if they do, they are hard-pressed to set aside the very powerful emotional and physical drives to get high. It's no wonder that the success rate for standard addiction treatment is generally acknowledged to be only somewhere between 20–30 percent. In light of these dismal statistics, health professionals and laypeople alike can't be blamed for concluding that addiction simply isn't treatable. Perhaps that's the reason that only 2.2 million of the estimated 17.6 million Americans suffering from alcohol abuse or dependence actually seek (or are pushed into) treatment programs.

New Understanding, New Medicines, New Hope

The good news is that, armed with this understanding of addiction as a brain disease requiring medical treatment, we are in a much better position to tackle the problem effectively. A key component of the new addiction treatment is the new anti-addiction medications designed to rebalance the brain's biochemistry. These medications in many cases make it almost impossible for those with addictions to experience a high, from the addictive substance they ingest, inject, or inhale. They help correct imbalances in dopamine and other essential neurotransmitters and accelerate healing of the physical damage in both the limbic region and the cortex. Once this damage has begun to heal, a person with addictions will find it much easier to learn, remember, and focus on the suggested cognitive and behavioral changes used in talking therapy and achieve longer-lasting sobriety. These medications have been scientifically proven to reduce substance use substantially. For example, in alcoholics the use of a form of naltrexone known as Vivitrol was able to reduce the median number of "drinking days" per month from 15.2 to 0.2.

The New Paradigm: Recovery Science–The Comprehensive Treatment Strategy

Thanks to modern medical science, we can take a much more effective approach to the problem of alcohol and drug addiction—a scientific, comprehensive approach that I call Recovery Science.

The key elements of the Recovery Science comprehensive treatment strategy is based on the understanding that addiction is a chronic brain disease which causes physical changes in the brain that sorely hamper therapy and that new medications can be used to augment therapy. But let me be perfectly clear about one thing: I'm not saying that the new medicines are a magical cure or that we can forget the other treatments, rather just the opposite is true. Talking therapies (including the 12-step programs) are still essential to the recovery process, as are mastering new coping skills and making permanent lifestyle modifications. Insulin alone isn't the solution for a diabetic, who must also learn how to eat a healthful diet, exercise regularly, remain slim, check his feet for cuts and sores that may become infected, and otherwise adhere to a good-health program. Neither are the new medications a simple solution to addiction. Addicts must learn to handle cravings, attend 12-step meetings regularly, and otherwise re-vamp their thinking, behavior, and lifestyle. However, the judicious use of new anti-addiction medicines can greatly enhance the ability to focus on and benefit from group and individual therapy and follow a 12-step program.

Why is all of this new information so important for you to understand? Actually, it is critical for you or your loved one to learn and know these con-cepts because most physicians and addiction treatment providers are either not aware of them or will not tell you about these important recovery tools. Either way, you will need to become the expert on hour to treat addiction success-fully—you need to learn and apply the "secret sauce"—the scientific findings. Luckily, the "secret sauce" is quite simple; let's review: 1) Alcohol and drug addiction is a chronic medical disease of the brain. Treat it as such and your chances of long term successful sobriety should sky rocket. 2) Your treatment program needs to be comprehensive, meaning it needs to include multiple elements; specifically, both anti-addiction and psychiatric medication (when appropriate), individual and group talking therapy to teach you healthy cop-ing skills, 12-step programs, wellness/nutrition programs (to help accelerate your brains' and body's healing), neurological evaluations to assess and better treat any brain injury, family therapy and spirituality, as well as other services depending on your specific life situation. This last point is extra important—all of these services need to be individualized to you and your life. Because there are different types of alcoholics and drug addicts, each with different sets of circumstances, recovery programs have to be personalized for you or your loved ones, just as cancer treatments are customized to different patients. That's it! You now have the "secret sauce". Understanding these concepts empowers you and makes you a better-educated consumer of addiction treatment services, so you or your loved ones can access the optimal combination of these services and have them personalized to your specific life situation, in order that they may afford you the highest chance for successful long-term sobriety.

View this book as your "road map" or your "playbook" that will empower you with the latest scientific tools and findings. Each of the chapters teaches you about one of these important areas and then you can go out and find these services for yourself or a loved one. You will most likely have to go to several different locations/providers in order to get all of them, but at least now you will know what to ask for and what you need.

Once we begin treating addiction as a chronic brain disease, we'll see a tremendous rise in the treatment success rate. Our new comprehensive approach will bring alcohol and drug addiction out of the closet, washing away the "stain of sin" and identifying it as a medical illness in need of treatment. With the stigma removed, more people will be willing to admit they need treatment, and the treatment they do receive will be much more likely to solve the problem.

Enter into Health

In the chapters that follow, you'll learn more about the effects of addiction and the optimal methods for treating it. This book is based on the Recovery Science anti-addiction program detailed on the EnterHealth.com website. Space limitations prevent me from going into as much detail about certain topics as I'd like, but at EnterHealth you'll find in-depth explanations of many of the topics covered in this book, as well as printable worksheets that will help you put the Recovery Science principles into practice. Utilizing the results of the latest research on clinical addiction treatment, EnterHealth's Advanced Recovery program offers ongoing personalized addiction education and treatment for people at any stage of recovery. This means that by accessing the website you can customize the information in this book to your own situation—a very powerful tool for recovery. Then, EnterHealth's Life Care program will show you how to apply these concepts to the lifelong process of recovery.

Simply go to www.EnterHealth.com/HealingtheAddictedBrain and begin exploring the educational area dedicated to this book. There is also a comprehensive area of the site where you can access innovative e-learning tools that provide in-depth addiction education and support to complement any treatment program. The website is also extremely helpful to family members of alcoholics and addicts who want to understand and support their loved ones' recovery.

In the chapters that follow, I'll take a detailed look at the disease of addiction, including the way the brain damage it causes distorts thinking in such a way that continuing to drink or use makes perfect sense to the addict. Chapters Two and Three introduce tools for identifying and converting the pro-addiction thoughts into pro-recovery thoughts, as well as techniques for extinguishing triggers and controlling cravings.

In Chapter Four I look at the new medicines that are revolutionizing addiction treatment, and in Chapter Five I discuss 12-step programs, one of the strongest tools for maintaining sobriety. You may be tempted to skip to Chapter Four to read about the medicines. That's understandable, but remember: even though the use of these medications can push the successful treatment rate up to 90 percent or more, they are only one element of a comprehensive addiction program. It is equally important to learn about lapses, dual diagnoses, family and health issues, 12-step support, and all the other components of long-term sobriety.

Chapters Six and Seven present ways to handle the anger, depression, and other problems that typically accompany addiction, while Chapter Eight offers ideas and encouragement for the families of addicts. Chapter Nine concludes discussion of handling addiction-related problems by presenting tools for preventing or dealing with lapses and relapses. The final three chapters look to the future, discussing ways to learn to enjoy sober life again, use food and nutrition to improve your health, and start living a truly recovered life, in which you can maintain your control over your addictive behaviors.

There are many ideas to absorb and new skills to master in recovery. It may seem like a lot to handle all at once. Yes, it can be overwhelming. *But I've seen many people break through to permanent sobriety when they follow all of these science-based recommendations.* Take it step by step, day by day. Expect the occasional setback; when it happens, remind yourself that you're human. Always keep your eye on the goal—there's an excellent chance you'll get there!

Key Points Review

- Addiction is a chronic medical illness that attacks the brain, damaging key parts of the cerebral cortex and limbic system.

- With standard traditional treatment, the chance of recovering from addiction and maintaining that recovery is 20–30 percent.

- With the new Recovery Science approach to treatment, the chance of recovering from addiction and maintaining that recovery can approach 90 percent.

- Seventy-five percent of alcoholics are not in treatment, even though alcoholism is nearly as life threatening as heart disease and cancer.

- Two myths have put a stranglehold on the development of effective new therapies for addiction: *addiction is a kind of "personality disease,"* and *"talking therapy" is the only significant treatment.*

- Addiction is not an "acute" (short-term) illness with a short-term solution.

- Like diabetes, asthma, and other chronic diseases, addiction can be controlled but never eliminated.

- Excessive ingestion of alcohol injures and shrinks a healthy, normal-sized brain.

- Much of the injury to the brain occurs in the frontal cortex, an area that plays an important role in memory, judgment, impulse control, problem solving, and other intellectual skills.

- Damage also occurs in the limbic region, a structure deep inside the brain that controls desires and the body's basic drives.

- Many of the forty different major neurotransmitter systems in the brain are disrupted by chronic alcohol or drug use.

- Chronic consumption of alcohol or drugs causes the release of overly abundant amounts of the neurotransmitters, including dopamine, which contribute to the feeling of being high and make you want to get high again.

- Talking therapies work, but *only* if the brain is willing and able to pay attention, listen, and remember. They do nothing to address the chronic brain damage.

- New anti-addiction medicines can help repair the addiction-inflicted brain damage and greatly enhance one's ability to focus on and benefit from group and individual therapy and follow a 12-step program.

- Sometimes medication works so well and so quickly that it seems like a "quick cure," but it is critical that the individual follow through with the comprehensive treatment model, including 12-step programs, psychiatric care, psychotherapy, wellness/nutrition/stress management, neuropsychological assessment, and family therapy in order to make lifestyle changes and learn new coping skills necessary to maintain sobriety.

- You can use www.EnterHealth.com/HealingtheAddictedBrain in partnership with this book to personalize the concepts presented here.

CHAPTER TWO

Changing Your Thoughts from Pro-Addiction to Pro-Recovery

People with addictions often have certain ideas about their substance of abuse, themselves, and the world around them that are fundamentally incorrect. We call these ideas "thought distortions." The addicted brain is full of distorted and irrational thoughts. Part of this is due to the process of addiction, which physically damages the brain, and part of it is due to the practice of addiction, which requires isolation, disengaging from normal, healthy emotions, rationalizing, and developing mental subterfuges, all of which make it more difficult to think clearly.

I saw a textbook case of the thought distortions that plague the addicted brain when Hank introduced himself at his very first group meeting. The handsome, apparently confident forty-seven-year-old sales manager began by insisting he didn't have a problem, even though his wife had encouraged him to get treatment. He went on to tell us that it was actually a *good* thing that he "popped a few" before sales meetings. Here's how his particular brand of thought distortion played out:

"We have at least ten meetings a week, and they're all very high-pressure with lots of money riding on them. If I take a few pills, I'm more re-laxed, which means I'll make a good impression, which is good for sales.

What's good for sales is good for my salary, and what's good for my salary is good for my family, so you could say that 'popping a few' is good for my family. And what am I doing that's so evil? Millions of people have a few drinks at lunch meetings every day. I do drugs instead of martinis, so I'm a loser/junkie/criminal and they're not?"

No, Hank wasn't a criminal. But he *was* good at rationalizing. So good, in fact, that he soon decided he could drop out of treatment. I heard later that he was rushed to the hospital, suffering from a nearly fatal overdose.

The Brain as a Battleground

Hank's rationalizations were common. Addicts who are practicing their addiction, as well as addicts newly in recovery, *truly believe* that they need or deserve to drink or use, and are *convinced* that those who try to help them are really harming them. They can't help but feel that way because their brains are literally damaged, and this damage makes it difficult for them to understand and accept healthful ideas and adopt healthful behaviors.

The addicted brain is a battleground between pro-addiction thoughts (thoughts that push you toward drinking or using) and pro-recovery thoughts (thoughts that help you stay sober). This ongoing struggle makes clear thinking difficult, and the brain often interprets uncomfortable or unpleasant feelings as cravings, sending its owner off in search of some form of substance for relief. This is one reason why it's so hard for an addict to stay focused on recovery.

These "dueling thoughts" (pro-addiction vs. pro-recovery thoughts) make it difficult for people like Terri, a thirty-two-year-old accountant, to stick to a recovery program.

"I want to be sober," she told me the first time I met her in my office. "I need to be sober or I'll lose everything." For Terri, "everything" meant her relationship with her boyfriend, Mark, and the possibility of becoming a partner in the firm. "But these thoughts in my head," she continued,

"keep going back and forth. I want to drink; I don't want to drink. I will follow my psychologist's advice for awhile, then say, 'Forget that head shrinker!' I'll try to avoid drinking by working twelve hours a day, then I realize that I can't possibly get through a day that long without a drink. I'll promise to do anything to stay sober and make Mark proud of me, then wonder why he can't understand what I'm going through and get off my back. Practically every thought I have seems to push the one I just had out of my head until I don't know what I'm thinking! It's like they're not even my thoughts. It's not me thinking in there."

The good news is that as you get sober, your thinking will begin to clear up. But getting back to "normal" thinking won't simply be a matter of waiting until the last remnants of alcohol or drugs have cleared from your brain, for the physical damage they caused can take months, years, or even decades to heal—or may never be completely healed. In a sense, you'll have to learn to think all over again, learn to control the harmful pro-addiction thoughts and replace them with healthy pro-recovery thoughts. And that takes time, determination, practice, and patience.

From Situation to Thoughts to Emotions to Behavior

Learning to think clearly begins with a true understanding of the nature of thoughts, emotions, and behavior and how they affect each other.

* *Thoughts* are created in the cortex, the rational part of the brain. Believe it or not, you have absolute control over your thoughts. While addiction "encourages" certain pro-addiction thoughts, it cannot *make* you think anything. Only you can formulate a thought. It's also important to realize that just because a thought has arisen, it is not necessarily true.

* *Emotions* are feelings like happiness, sadness, anger, fear, or longing. Alcohol and drugs alter your emotions by changing the way your

brain works. In the early phases of recovery, you may find it difficult to identify your emotions correctly, because the addictive substance has been blotting them out for so long. Then, as you begin to get sober, you'll start experiencing the normal emotions of everyday life, which can be a real shock. All kinds of emotions will arise, whether you want them to or not. And while you can't stop experiencing emotions, you can control their impact on your behavior.

• *Behavior* is the sum total of your actions, what you actually do in specific situations. Work and play are behaviors. Drinking alcohol and using drugs are behaviors, and so is going to a treatment session or an AA meeting. Behavior is triggered by thoughts and emotions. A certain situation may stimulate particular thoughts in your brain, which create various emotions, which in turn produce behaviors. This diagram illustrates the progression:

Situation → Thoughts → Emotions → Behavior

To illustrate, imagine you're headed to a party (the situation). You don't know who will be at this party, and you imagine that you won't fit in (thought). This makes you feel anxious (emotion), so you down a few beers (behavior) before you leave the house. This progression from situation to thoughts to emotions to behavior may seem inevitable, but remember that you *can* control your thoughts. You may be stuck with the situation, but if you control the harmful thoughts that trigger the negative emotions, you can stop the pro-addiction behaviors.

The Inaccurate and Irrational Thinking of Addiction

Inaccurate pro-addiction thoughts are by definition invalid, although they seem absolutely true to the addicted person. They are based on the belief that you will fail or get hurt and the only way to succeed, or at least avoid the pain of failure, is to blot out the situation or the feelings by drinking alcohol or using drugs. For example, you might think, "I'll lose all my friends if I go into this recovery program." This thought is inaccurate: your true friends will want you to become healthy again. But you may continue to believe this pro-addiction thought because it gives you a reason to avoid the possibility of failure.

People with addictions get caught in cycles of pro-addiction thinking that lead to unpleasant emotions that lead to harmful pro-addiction behaviors. In most cases, they're not even aware of what's happening. Here are some common inaccurate, pro-addiction thoughts:

- I can't get through this without alcohol or drugs.

- Using is the only way I'll be creative and productive.

- When I get angry, the only way to calm down is to drink or use.

- If I don't have a drink right now, I'll die from these horrible cravings.

- It's okay if I disappoint the kid by not showing up at his party; he'll get over it.

- I'll be all right in the long run because they'll probably invent a pill to cure addiction soon.

- I can't relax without alcohol or drugs.

- Getting stoned isn't really harming my job/family/life.

- Those docs don't know what they're talking about. Why should I listen to them?

- My girlfriend/boyfriend thinks I'm cute when I'm drunk.

- There's nothing wrong with me; it's everyone else.

- I can stop whenever I want.

When you're in the grip of pro-addiction thoughts like these, you experience powerful negative emotions that can push you into drinking or using behaviors. And after a while, you may go straight to drinking or using without even waiting for the negative thoughts or emotions to arise. For example, as soon as Terri would find out that she'd have to attend a family party, she'd immediately knock back a few beers to ward off the uncomfortable feelings she knew would arise when she saw certain family members.

Do You Have Inaccurate, Pro-Addiction Thoughts?

Read each statement and rate it as follows:

1	2	3	4	5	6	7
Disagree	Disagree	Disagree	Neutral	Agree	Agree	Agree
Totally	Strongly	Slightly		Slightly	Strongly	Totally

_____ 1. Life without drinking or using is boring.

_____ 2. Drinking or using is the only way to increase my creativity and productivity.

_____ 3. I can't function without alcohol or drugs.

_____ 4. Using drugs or alcohol is my way of coping with the pain in my life.

_____ 5. I'm not ready to stop drinking or using.

_____ 6. It's the urges and cravings that make me drink or use.

_____ 7. Even if I stop drinking or using, my life won't get any better.

_____ 8. The only way to deal with my anger is by drinking or using.

_____ 9. Life would be depressing if I stopped drinking or using.

_____ 10. I don't deserve to recover from alcohol or drug use.

_____ 11. I'm not strong enough to stop.

_____ 12. I could not be social without drinking or using.

_____ 13. Substance use is not a problem for me.

_____ 14. My substance use is caused by someone else (boss, spouse, boyfriend/girlfriend, family member).

_____ 15. Problems with alcohol or drugs are caused by genetics.

_____ 16. I can't relax without alcohol or drugs.

_____ 17. Having a problem with alcohol or drugs means I am fundamentally a bad person.

_____ 18. I can't control my anxiety without drinking or using drugs.

_____ 19. My life means nothing unless I drink or use.

Any item marked with a 6 or a 7 indicates a seriously inaccurate pro-addiction thought that will increase the likelihood of relapse. Use these 6s and 7s as examples to create more accurate, pro-recovery thoughts later in the chapter.

Addiction not only causes but *thrives* on inaccurate, pro-addiction thoughts, which means it's practically inevitable that you'll experience fearful emotions and harmful behavior. But until you realize that you have such thoughts, you can't start to change them.

Identifying Inaccurate Thinking

To discover the inaccuracies in your own thinking, it's extremely important that you get into the habit of writing out your thoughts on a regular basis. Buy yourself an 8″ x 10″ notebook (your "Thought Notebook"), and designate fifteen to thirty minutes a day to write out the thoughts you've had in the previous twenty-four hours, especially those that brought up uncomfortable emotions or preceded cravings for drugs or alcohol. Don't try to keep track of these thoughts in your head—putting them on paper will make it much easier to find any logical flaws in your thinking. As you add to your Thought Notebook over time, continually review what you've written during days past to see if you can gain insight into the ways that your thoughts affect your feelings and behaviors. (See Melanie's story below.)

Thinking about what was happening at the time may help you recall the accompanying thoughts. So if you can't remember the thoughts that immediately preceded negative emotions or a relapse into addictive behaviors, think about the situations you faced at the time. Then try to recall what you thought and how you felt. You may also find it helpful to work backward from the emotion to the thought. Identify an uncomfortable emotion that you had recently—for example, anger, sadness, or anxiety—then try and figure out what you were thinking that brought on that emotion. Because pro-addiction thoughts occur so quickly (often too quickly to recognize early in your recovery), it can sometimes be easier to identify the uncomfortable emotions.

One of my patients, Melanie, a young sales clerk, kept ignoring my request that she write down her pro-addiction thoughts as they popped up during the day. "I don't have many," she laughed, noting that it was silly for her to think thoughts that would keep her addiction in play. After all, she wanted to get better, not worse. I finally insisted that she write down her pro-addiction thoughts. She agreed, but added that I'd be disappointed when I saw how small her list would be.

Two weeks later she practically ran into my office, waving a notepad in the air, and shouted, "My God, look at this! I can't believe how scared I am! I never thought I was scared, but listen to what I put down here for my thoughts today." She began to read:

- *Walking out of house, thinking I'll miss the train and be late.*
- *Walking into work, thinking my outfit isn't right and people will notice.*

- *Talking to customers, thinking I'll say something silly every time and they'll think I'm an idiot.*
- *Putting up the display like the boss told me, thinking I'll do it wrong and he'll yell at me.*
- *Going to lunch with girlfriends at work, thinking I'll say or do something stupid and they'll laugh at me.*
- *Going on first date with guy from the dating service, thinking he'll take one look at me and not like me.*

"I didn't have a single good thought about myself all day long! And I didn't even know it!"

Identifying Thought Inaccuracies

Once you've begun to zero in on your thoughts via the Thought Notebook, you can start to look for inaccuracies in your reasoning. People tend to experience the same kinds of thought inaccuracies over and over. Once you have identified your own specific types of distortions, you can be on the lookout for them. Just increasing your awareness will make it easier for you to recognize such thoughts and replace them with healthier, more accurate thoughts. Listed below are some well-known thought inaccuracies that affect many people with addictions. Read through the following categories of inaccuracy, and see which ones apply to you.

All-or-Nothing Thinking

Thought: "Either I'm perfect or I'm a failure. Either I'm good or I'm bad. Either I'm really wonderful or completely terrible."

Truth: People are naturally imperfect, which is why thinking these thoughts sets you up for failure. Those with this mind-set often go on a binge when they make the tiniest mistake. Realize that success comes in degrees and that you can always pull back from the edge, even if (and especially when) you've stepped over the line.

Need for Distraction or Comfort

Thought: "If I have a drink (or a hit), I'll feel better."

Truth: Addictive behaviors only mask trouble and are poor substitutes for dealing with life directly. Not only do they distract you from what you should be focusing on, they destroy your mental and physical health, relationships, career, and financial status.

Need for Instant Gratification

Thought: "I have to change the way I feel right *now*. I can't wait another second."

Truth: Drinking or using may be a short-term solution to bad feelings, but the bad feelings it causes in the long run are much, much worse. Waiting out an urge or a craving is the best way to weaken the power of future cravings.

Overgeneralizing

Thought: "I really tied one on last night. I'll never be able to control my addiction."

Truth: This is a broad conclusion based on a single incident. One event doesn't predict the outcome.

Catastrophizing

Thought: "I got drunk last night and yelled at my kids. Now they'll hate me forever."

Truth: You're focusing on the worst-case scenario. The chances of this happening are less than zero, so don't automatically assume the worst.

Rationalizing

Thought: "I use drugs because I was an abused child."

Truth: Your background may have had something to do with the reason you developed an addiction, but it is no excuse for keeping the addiction in play.

Personal Ineffectiveness

Thought: "I know I should give up drinking/drugs. I just can't make myself do it."

Truth: You can do more than you think you can. Try harder, and congratulate yourself for each tiny success.

Confusing Your Behavior with Your Worth

Thought: "I use drugs, therefore I am worthless scum."

Truth: Your actions and your worth as a human being are two different things. You are not what you do. However, you can change your behavior and your life for the better.

Challenging the Inaccuracies

Look over the thoughts in your Thought Notebook, and pick out one or two that you think might be distorted. Then challenge the accuracy of those thoughts by asking yourself the six questions listed below and thinking through the answers.

Six-Question Test of Thought Accuracy

   1. What concrete factual evidence supports or refutes this thought?

   2.   Are there other ways I could view the situation?

   3.   What is the worst thing that could happen?

   4.   What is the best thing that could happen?

   5. Realistically speaking, what is most likely to happen?

   6.   Is this thought inaccurate? If so, which category of inaccuracy?

For example, suppose you are wrestling with this thought: "I have to go to a big party with a ton of strangers, I'm really bad at mingling, no one will talk to me, and I'll have a miserable time." Is this an inaccurate thought? Let's ask the six questions and find out.

1. What concrete factual evidence supports or refutes this thought?

It's true that I'm not comfortable mixing. However, there's no proof that I'm any worse at mingling than most other people. There will probably be plenty of uncomfortable people there who are just dying to talk to someone—maybe even me! There's no real reason why I should be destined to have a miserable time at the party.

2. Are there other ways I could view this situation?

This party could be a good opportunity to practice mingling. I may be able to have a good time just listening to others talking, getting into the music, eating good food, and enjoying the scenery.

3. What is the worst thing that could happen?

I'll be bored and sneak out early.

4. What is the best thing that could happen?

I'll meet some interesting people, have some good conversations, or see some old friends.

5. Realistically speaking, what is most likely to happen?

The party won't be great, but it won't be terrible either. I'll get a little better at handling parties each time I go, and someday I'll actually be comfortable mingling with strangers.

6. Is this an inaccurate thought? If so, which category of inaccuracy?

This inaccurate thought is an example of personal ineffectiveness—assuming that something is just too hard and can't be accomplished. I need to try harder.

Working through these six questions can help you develop more accurate, logical thoughts, such as "This party may be fun, but if it's not, I'll practice mingling." If you find it hard to shake an inaccurate thought even after you've gone through the process described above, ask someone you trust if they can help you see the distortion and change it to an accurate thought. Getting someone else's input when evaluating inaccurate thoughts can be a very effective tool.

Six-Question Test of Thought Accuracy

Here's a blank Six-Question Test of Thought Accuracy you can use to check for inaccurate thinking. Make copies of the blank form and fill it in a couple times a week to check your thinking.

I thought that _____

_____

_____

1) What concrete factual evidence supports or refutes this thought?

_____

_____

_____

2) Are there other ways I could view the situation?

_____

_____

_____

3) What is the worst thing that could happen?

_____

_____

_____

4) What is the best thing that could happen?

_____

_____

_____

5) Realistically speaking, what is most likely to happen?

_____

_____

_____

6) Is this thought inaccurate? If so, which category of inaccuracy?

_____

_____

_____

Additional Questions to Test Thought Accuracy

Taking the process further, you can ask yourself these questions when examining the accuracy of your thoughts:

1. Am I assuming every situation is the same?

Are you taking into consideration the specific situation, including differing locations, relationships, times, and so on? For example, the fact that you gave in and used drugs after your mother died doesn't mean that you'll give in and use every time you face a difficult emotional situation.

2. Am I focusing on irrelevant factors?

Are you trying to defend a negative attitude about life by asking things like, "What about Darfur and starving children?" Yes, there is misery and evil in the world but that has nothing to do with your present situation, and it's no excuse for negative thinking.

3. *Am I overlooking my strengths?*

When people feel bad, they tend to overlook their past successes. Reminding yourself of how well you've done in the past is an excellent way to increase confidence in your ability to handle present problems.

4. *How would I look at this if I weren't feeling so bad?*

You may, for example, think that your current withdrawal symptoms are the worst thing in the world. But if you weren't feeling so bad physically, you might be able to see that this is just a difficult passage on the road to a wonderful new life.

5. *What can I do to solve the problem?*

Are your thoughts encouraging problem blocking instead of problem solving? If your children are fighting and the plumbing is stopped up, thinking about the unfairness of it all won't solve the problem. Thinking about possible solutions is a lot more likely to lead to a happy resolution.

6. *Am I asking myself questions that have no answers?*

If you're focusing on questions like "How can I redo the past?" or "How can I become someone different?" you're just spinning your wheels. Asking yourself unanswerable questions is another way of demanding that the world be different than it is.

7. *What are the advantages and disadvantages of thinking this way?*

Ask yourself if there are any advantages in thinking, "I'm a loser, and I'll never get sober." Probably not. Instead, there's a major disadvantage: this kind of thinking can stop you from taking positive steps toward getting sober.

8. *What difference will this make in a week, a year, or ten years from now?*
Suppose you have a small relapse, then get right back on the wagon. Ten years from now, will anyone remember, let alone care, about your little relapse?

Substituting Healthy Thoughts for Inaccurate Thoughts

Now that you have identified some of your inaccurate thoughts, try rewriting them to reflect a healthier, more accurate way of thinking. Here are some examples of inaccurate, pro-addiction thoughts and more accurate, pro-recovery thoughts.

Pro-Addiction Thought, Pro-Recovery Response	
INACCURATE PRO-ADDICTION THOUGHT	**MORE ACCURATE PRO-RECOVERY RESPONSE**
I'm going to fail.	I'll probably do all right, but even if I don't, it's not the end of the world.
I'm afraid of social situations.	Nothing at a social event is truly dangerous, so nothing really serious will happen to me.
I need to drink or use to feel good.	There are lots of ways to feel good that don't involve drinking or using: sitting in a jacuzzi, seeing a funny movie, playing my favorite sport, hanging out with good (sober) friends.
I can't be social without drinking or using.	If I can talk about the weather, sports, food, movies or any other simple topic, I can be social.
I've done a lot of crappy things to my family, so they'll always hate me.	I certainly have amends to make, but my family will most likely welcome me back.

| It's the urges and cravings that make me drink. | The urges and cravings are there, but they will go away if I just wait them out. Meanwhile, I can develop new ways of thinking about and responding to them. With time, patience and practice, I can learn to overcome them. |
| I messed up and used yesterday. I might as well give up trying to get sober. | No one is perfect, we all backslide from time to time. I've made a mistake. I'll learn from it and move on. |

Using the form below, write out six of your own inaccurate, pro-addiction thoughts, then substitute a more accurate pro-recovery response for each one. (Make several copies of this form so you can check and correct your thoughts several times a week.)

Pro-Addiction Thought, Pro-Recovery Response Worksheet

INACCURATE PRO-ADDICTION THOUGHT	MORE ACCURATE PRO-RECOVERY RESPONSE
1)	
2)	
3)	
4)	
5)	
6)	

I remember how pleased my patient Steve was when he reported his success. It took him awhile, but Steve, a thirtyish graphic artist, developed the habit of implanting a pro-recovery thought in his mind before an inaccurate, pro-addiction one had time to arise. For example, as soon as he was invited to a party, Steve would think, "Good chance to meet people, maybe make a business contact." As soon as he got a new commission, he would consciously think, "Another chance to shine." Upon setting up a date with a new woman, he would tell himself, "The chances of being charming are excellent; the chances of getting some action are good."

He was not always entirely successful, of course, but most of the time Steve found he could "push" the good thought into place before the bad one arrived. It was wonderful to see this young man sweeping his pro-addiction thinking away after eight years of off-and-on drug use punctuated by stays in treatment centers.

Practice, Practice, Practice

You'll need to practice identifying, writing down, and correcting inaccurate, pro-addiction thinking on a daily basis in order to enjoy optimal results. Try to do so while you're calm—don't wait until a crisis hits! Be aware that your addiction isn't the only source of thought inaccuracies: anxiety, depression, grief, and other unhappy emotions also cause them. But all inaccurate thoughts can be dangerous, so be on the lookout for them, especially during stressful times. Chances are, you'll never eliminate all of your pro-addiction thoughts, but that's normal. The point is for your pro-recovery thoughts to far outnumber your pro-addiction ones.

Key Points Review

- The brain of an addict or a person in recovery is a battleground for pro-addiction and pro-recovery thoughts. This can make you feel like you're crazy, but it's completely normal.

- You are the only one who puts thoughts into your head, which means that you are in control of your thinking.

- Situation → Thoughts → Emotion → Behavior: A situation may stimulate thoughts in your brain, which create various emotions, which in turn produce behaviors.

- Healthy, accurate thoughts help you refrain from drinking or using.

- Not every thought you think is true, and not every feeling is an accurate response to a given situation.

- When you are addicted or are in the early phases of recovery, many of your thoughts and feelings will be inaccurate or distorted.

- With practice, you can identify and change the inaccurate, pro-addiction thoughts that lead to unhappy emotions and unhealthy behaviors.

- Inaccurate, pro-addiction thoughts can be converted into more accurate thoughts by applying common sense and logical thinking.

- Writing down your thoughts will help you find the logical flaws and inaccuracies that encourage addiction. The Six Question Test of Thought Accuracy can be very helpful in this important process.

- Once you identify pro-addiction thinking, you can take steps to change it to pro-recovery thinking.

- It usually helps to talk with someone about a particular pro-addiction thought, as they can help point out the inaccuracies with it, and then it is easy to change it into a pro-recovery thought.

CHAPTER THREE

Combating Triggers and Cravings

It doesn't take much to make you want to drink or use again.

A stray thought can trigger a craving. Or the urge might strike when you're fighting with your ex-spouse, walking by a bar where you used to drink, getting chewed out by your boss, or remembering something unpleasant from your childhood. A thousand things can arouse the urge to drink or use again.

A lot of people will tell you to avoid these people and situations, and sometimes this well-meaning advice can become overwhelming. But trying to avoid all of these situations, thoughts, or people is not only impractical, it's impossible. Everyday things like being home alone, getting your paycheck, driving through a specific neighborhood, hearing a certain song, going to an ATM, and walking into a bathroom can all set you off, and you'll just have to live with many of them. The trick is learning to identify and "deactivate" your triggers before you're propelled into using. And you must have a plan in place to handle those cravings that do arise.

What Are Triggers?

A trigger is an idea, concept, person, place, thing, or emotional state that stimulates the urge to drink or use. Almost anything can serve as a trigger, even "good" things like planning your spouse's birthday party, taking your children to the park, or finding that you have a little spare cash. The trigger itself may appear to be completely harmless, but the associations it creates in your mind can greatly increase the likelihood that you'll start drinking or using again. Some triggers are obvious, but others can be hidden and very difficult to identify. Here are some common triggers:

- *People*—friends, coworkers, spouse/lover, family members, drug dealers, employer, dates, neighbors

- *Places*—certain neighborhoods, a friend's home, bars and clubs, hotels, your worksite, concerts, a certain freeway exit, bathrooms, your stash storage place, school, downtown

- *Events*—group meetings, parties, payday, calls from creditors, going out, anniversaries, holidays, situations that involve meeting new people

- *Objects*—paraphernalia, magazines, pornography, movies, television, cash, credit cards, ATMs, the telephone you used to call your dealer, any other item that reminds you of when you were drinking or using

- *Behaviors and activities*—listening to certain music, going on a date, having sex, going out to eat, going dancing, being home alone, hanging out with friends, driving, arguing, paying bills

- *Emotions or feelings*—fear, anxiety, guilt, irritation, anger, overconfidence, hate, jealousy, shame, depression, inadequacy, feeling overwhelmed, feeling rejected, feeling criticized, boredom, insecurity, nervousness, sadness, embarrassment, loneliness, fatigue, frustration, neglect, feeling relaxed, feeling pressured, excitement, happiness, hopefulness, passion, confidence, sexual arousal

- *Uncomfortable body sensations*—stomach discomfort, familiar pain from an old injury, new pain, onset of a disease, withdrawal symptoms

In short, triggers can be any item, person, place, situation, thought, or emotion that begins the cycle of destructive thinking that leads to drinking or using. If something—*anything*—brings up thoughts such as these, it is a trigger:

- "I can't deal with this…"
- "I need to get away…"
- "I need to forget…"
- "Using would be a blast…"

Lisa, a twenty-two-year-old woman attending a high-profile university, was about eighteen months behind in her studies and had flunked six courses during the previous couple of years due to her abuse of alcohol. She had great trouble concentrating on her studies and remembering facts. Unfortunately, as her frustrations grew and her self-esteem plummeted, her alcohol intake increased. She lived in a sorority house where she regularly sat in the hall and drank with some of her sorority sisters in the evening. Thursday through Sunday nights she drank with various guys from a nearby fraternity before hitting the bar scene. And she often drank an entire bottle of wine by herself in the late evenings when she was supposed to be studying.

Most mornings Lisa woke up with a hangover, which would prompt her to swear off drinking for the next week. But usually by the time the afternoon rolled around, Lisa would run into one of her drinking buddies who'd suggest they go grab some beers or knock back a few shots. And off she'd go on another drinking binge.

Lisa's triggers were many and varied: low self-esteem, problems with her schoolwork, the hallway of her sorority house, certain sorority sisters, the guys at the nearby fraternity house, the local bar scene, various drinking buddies, and even her very own room late at night. No wonder she found herself unable to stop.

The list of potential triggers can be divided numerous ways: the external (people, places, events, objects, behaviors, and activities) and the internal (negative, normal, and positive feelings), the tangible and the intangible, the physical and the emotional, the real and the imagined. But whatever the form or category, a trigger leads to irrational thinking and is a very powerful incentive to slide or backslide into alcohol or drug use.

What Are Cravings?

A craving is a physical urge or compulsion to drink or use that is generated in the brain and experienced physically. Both mind and body "scream" at you unmercifully to drink or use—right now! Cravings can be extremely hard to control when they're in full swing, but once you gain an understanding of how and why they happen, you'll be much better prepared to ward them off or at least nip them in the bud.

John, a fifty-five-year-old sound editor, had been drinking since he was fifteen years old. Although he could see that alcohol was messing up his life, he really liked to drink. It tasted good, it smelled good, and it made him feel good. And when he went without it for any length of time, he really suffered. He described his cravings as having butterflies in his stomach and the taste of alcohol in his mouth. He looked forward to the happy, relaxed way he was going to feel after a few beers and the way his problems just seemed to melt away. He said he could even get himself to feel a little "buzzed" without drinking any alcohol; it was like a "pre-buzz." I explained to John that all of these symptoms, as well as many others, are generated by the neurochemical stimulation of certain deep brain control centers when specific triggers are encountered. They are physiological symptoms generated by the brain.

Take the following quiz to find out how much you know about cravings. Rate each of the following statements:

What Are Cravings to Me?

1	2	3	4	5	6	7
Disagree Totally	Disagree Strongly	Disagree Slightly	Neutral	Agree Slightly	Agree Strongly	Agree Totally

_____ 1. The craving is a physical reaction; therefore, I can't do anything about it.

_____ 2. If I don't stop the cravings, they will get worse.

_____ 3. Cravings can drive a person crazy.

_____ 4. The craving makes me use alcohol or drugs.

_____ 5. I'll always have cravings for alcohol or drugs.

_____ 6. I don't have any control over the cravings.

_____ 7. Once the cravings start, I have no control over my behavior.

_____ 8. I'll have cravings for alcohol or drugs for the rest of my life.

_____ 9. I can't stand the physical symptoms I have while craving alcohol or drugs.

_____ 10. The craving is my punishment for using alcohol or drugs.

_____ 11. If you have never used alcohol or drugs, you have no idea what the craving is like, and you can't expect me to resist.

_____ 12. The images and thoughts I have while craving alcohol or drugs are out of my control.

_____ 13. The cravings make me so nervous, I can't stand it.

_____ 14. I'll never be prepared to handle the cravings.

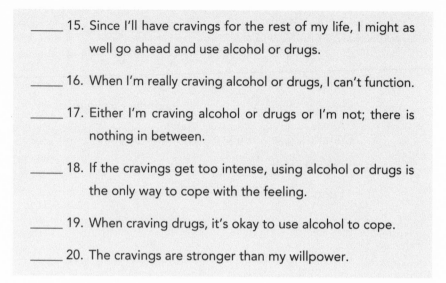

_____ 15. Since I'll have cravings for the rest of my life, I might as well go ahead and use alcohol or drugs.

_____ 16. When I'm really craving alcohol or drugs, I can't function.

_____ 17. Either I'm craving alcohol or drugs or I'm not; there is nothing in between.

_____ 18. If the cravings get too intense, using alcohol or drugs is the only way to cope with the feeling.

_____ 19. When craving drugs, it's okay to use alcohol to cope.

_____ 20. The cravings are stronger than my willpower.

If you gave any answer other than 1, you are misinformed! While it's true that you cannot prevent cravings from arising, you *can* control whether you will respond by drinking or using. The startling fact is people in recovery typically give in to only about 5 percent of their cravings! That means that *95 percent of the time, you will not drink or use in response to a craving.* That means that you can already resist just about all of your cravings—and with work and time, you can learn to resist the rest. How can this be true? Think about it—you might get a craving in a bus on the way to work, or sitting in the pew with your family on both sides of you, or at the end of the month when you have no money. In all of these situations, you have a craving but can't get to the substance and the craving passes. Remember that 95 percent figure. Write it down on a piece of paper, carry it with you, and look at it often.

How Do Triggers Produce Cravings?

You use alcohol or drugs to generate the "good" feelings we call "euphoria" or a "high." These substances stimulate the brain's "reward" system by activating a neurotransmitter called dopamine. The dopamine circuits are surrounded by the brain's hippocampus, which creates new memories, and the limbic system, which governs emotions. When alcohol or drugs activate the dopamine system, the hippocampus "switches on," ensuring that you will remember everything about the experience very clearly—not only the high, but also the people, places, objects, smells, and tastes associated with it (your trigger). The limbic system, for its part, contributes a strong emotional response to the mix. When you later come across the people, places, things, or emotional states related to your drug or alcohol use, your hippocampus activates the dopamine system to let you know that you are about to experience a very good feeling. This can arouse thoughts about drinking or using and a very strong emotional urge to do so.

Making matters worse, alcohol and drugs can damage the hippocampus, the limbic system, and other parts of the inner brain. When these areas are damaged, the delicate balance between neurotransmitters is upset, and your brain's ability to understand and respond to stimuli is weakened. In essence, these substances can "short circuit" your brain, causing it to send out inaccurate signals or false alarms, telling your body that something is good when it is not, or bad when it is really good. *Once the brain has been damaged by alcohol or drugs, these signals will continue racing through your head, urging you to drink or use even when there is no substance in sight.* Even if you're abstaining and trying hard to remain sober, your brain will continue to give you the wrong messages. These wayward signals from malfunctioning parts of your inner brain will "battle" with the logical reasons why you should abstain offered up by your cerebral cortex, the rational part of your brain. Which wins? That depends on what you do when the urge to drink or use arises and what you do to prevent these urges from arising in the first place.

In short, your cravings are not simply idle desires floating through your mind: they are hardwired into your brain, are part of your neural circuitry. Even if you have a strong desire to stay sober or clean, when you're exposed to a trigger, memory and dopamine circuits activate automatically, and you have to fight off the urge to drink or use (craving).

Classical Conditioning and Pavlov's Dog

Many people in recovery ask themselves, "How in the world did I wind up with so many triggers?" The answer is something called "classical conditioning."

Classical conditioning is a concept first discovered by Pavlov, a Russian scientist who conducted his famous experiment involving dogs. He used the visual trigger of a piece of steak to cause the dogs to produce saliva. Pavlov then rang a bell every time he gave the dogs steak, thus linking the sight of the steak to the sound of the bell in the dogs' brains. Eventually the dogs began to salivate when they heard the bell, even if there was no meat. In their brains, the reward (eating the meat) was paired with the sound of the bell.

The physiological and brain-driven phenomenon of classical conditioning is exactly what happens when triggers are created. You use alcohol or drugs to get a high. The euphoria becomes linked to anything you are looking at, smelling, hearing, touching, or feeling during or just before the use, and is programmed into your memory circuits. Thus, whenever you come across the people, places, feelings, or events associated with drug or alcohol use, your dopamine circuits become activated, letting you know that something very pleasurable is about to happen.

What Are Your Triggers?

Some triggers—the sight of an alcoholic drink or someone using crack cocaine—affect just about all drinkers or users, but the majority of triggers are personalized. What sets you off? On the other hand, what helps keep you in line? The following exercise can help you find out.

1) Make a list of the places where you are most likely to use alcohol or drugs.

_____

_____

_____

2) Make a list of the people with whom you are most likely to use alcohol or drugs.

_____

_____

_____

3) Make a list of the times of day when you are most likely to use alcohol or drugs.

_____

_____

_____

4) Make a list of activities that increase the likelihood you will use alcohol or drugs.

_____

_____

_____

5) Make a list of the places where you are unlikely to use alcohol or drugs.

_____

_____

_____

6) Make a list of the people with whom you are unlikely to use alcohol or drugs.

_____

_____

_____

7) Make a list of the times or days when you are unlikely to use alcohol or drugs.

_____

_____

_____

8) Make a list of the activities that decrease the likelihood you will use alcohol or drugs.

_____

_____

_____

The places, people, times, and activities in numbers 1 through 4 are danger zones for you, while those in numbers 5 through 8 are your safe areas. Spend as much time as reasonably possible in your safe areas during the early stages of your recovery. The more you are able to avoid your danger zones, the fewer triggers you will encounter and the easier it will be to maintain your sobriety.

 It's crucial that you identify, in very specific terms, the people, places, things, situations, thoughts, or emotions that trigger your urge to drink or use. For help developing your specific list of triggers, see the "Your Trigger Inventory" worksheet on www.EnterHealth.com/HealingtheAddictedBrain.

Charting Your Triggers

Most people are unaware that their thoughts about drinking or using have arisen from a trigger, and that these thoughts can incite addictive behaviors. Instead, they believe that these thoughts are inevitable and always irresistible. This tends to make them feel like there's no point in even trying to resist using. But if they understood how the trigger or craving mechanism triggered their behaviors, they would realize that they *can* control their actions, beat the craving, and *can* remain sober.

Chart the entire process, from trigger to thought to use; this will increase your understanding of the process. (It will give you something to be proud of as you track your successes in learning to control triggers.) Here's a sample Daily Trigger Chart, showing how a situation triggers thoughts or feelings, which lead to behaviors and their consequences:

Daily Trigger Chart				
Situation (Trigger)	Thoughts and Feelings	Behavior	Positive Consequences	Negative Consequences
A friend comes to my apartment with some coke.	Looks like good stuff. Could really get high. I deserve a break.	Do half gram of coke, then another gram.	Got really high. Don't remember much about the evening, but must have had fun.	Blew $300. Late to work next day. Missed important meeting. Supervisor wrote up reprimand for my file. Said one more tardy or missed meeting and he is going to let me go.

| After work, guys say "Let's go to the bar." | I know I should go home. I'm tired but know that I'll do some coke and that will help. | Go to bar. Drink a few beers. Shoot half gram. | Beers mellowed me out after a long day at work, but felt pretty sleepy as the night went along. The coke helped pick me up. | Wife was mad. Blew $75. Arm is sore. Have a horrible hangover. Feel sick to my stomach. Head is about to explode. |
| Saturday night | Time to party, feel like getting high. Staying home will be boring. | Go over to Tom's apartment. Get a few six-packs. Buy an eight-ball. High till 3 a.m. | Good coke, got really high. Met some new folks, but can't remember who they are. | Blew $200. Wrecked car on the way home. Arm sore. Missed kid's game in the a.m. Wife really mad and threatening to take the kids and leave me. |

 You'll find a printable copy of the "Daily Trigger Chart" on www.EnterHealth.com/HealingtheAddictedBrain. Print out several copies, and chart your triggers and responses every day, as often as they arise.

How to Handle Your Triggers

There are two main ways to handle triggers: avoid them (whenever possible) and extinguish them. Obviously, staying away from the ideas, people, places, and emotional states that inflame the urge to use is just good sense. While this isn't always possible, most people find that they can cut back on their exposure to triggers quite a bit.

As for extinguishing triggers, the memory circuits can actually be reprogrammed once the brain realizes that contact with the trigger no longer produces a high. But here's the catch: the only way you can accomplish this is by *consistently resisting the urge to use* when you're exposed to a trigger.

Avoiding Your Triggers

Here are some excellent suggestions for keeping triggers at bay:

- Stay away from drinking/drugging buddies.
- Stay away from old "using buildings" and "using neighborhoods."
- Find new restaurants, coffee shops, movie theaters, and other places to enjoy.
- Ask your spouse or significant other to handle the bills or use the ATM for you.
- Throw away any drug paraphernalia.
- Avoid arguments.
- As much as possible, stay away from people or events that upset you.
- Buy a new couch or other furniture to replace the "using piece."
- Take new routes to work.
- If you know that an upcoming event, such as a wedding or dinner, will trigger alcohol or drug use, do *not* go.
- If you are in a situation that seems to be triggering dangerous thoughts about drinking or using, leave immediately!
- If someone offers you a drink or a drug, just say, "No, thanks." You don't have to explain why, but if you do, simply say that you have a problem with alcohol or drugs or that you no longer drink or use.
- Even better, be proactive and ask people *not* to offer you alcohol or drugs.

After many discussions, Lisa, the alcoholic college student, understood the critical relationship between the triggers in her environment and her cravings. She made a concerted effort to avoid as many of them as she possibly could by making a list of her triggers, then finding ways to eliminate or steer clear of them. For example, she moved out of the sorority house and stopped visiting the guys at the fraternity house. She stopped hanging out with her sorority sisters who liked to drink and avoided the local bar scene. She also set aside time to study earlier in the day when she was fresh and more able to concentrate, and she did the bulk of her studying in the library. By cutting back drastically on her exposure to triggers, Lisa found that she was able to stop drinking completely without much trouble. Not only did her drinking problem subside, her memory and her school performance improved markedly.

Extinguishing Your Triggers

If it were possible to avoid all your triggers, the path to recovery would be smoother and shorter than it actually is. Unfortunately, triggers are unavoidable and unpredictable. You may encounter six one day and thirty the next; one trigger may produce a moderate yet manageable desire to drink or use, but the very next an irresistible craving. For that reason, you must learn to extinguish your triggers, to take away their power by not drinking or using when you encounter them.

If you continually resist the urge to drink or use when exposed to a trigger, your body and the hippocampal system in your brain will come to understand that the trigger is not a sign of good things to come. The dopamine system will no longer be automatically activated, and eventually the trigger will fail to produce a craving. That's why cravings become weaker the longer you stay sober.

Of course, resisting can be difficult. Sometimes cravings are so overwhelming, it seems impossible not to give in to them. That's when taking one of the safe, nonaddicting medications that reduce cravings can be particularly helpful. Used appropriately, these medications can decrease or even completely obliterate cravings within a few days to a few weeks. Other medicines appear to reprogram the addiction-damaged brain circuits, neutralizing the trigger's effects almost immediately. (See Chapter Four for a discussion of the anti-addiction medications.)

A key point regarding the type of treatment: it's best to extinguish as many triggers as you can, as soon as possible, but that requires exposure. If you're in an outpatient treatment program and living at home, you'll likely have this exposure. But if you're in a residential or inpatient treatment program, you're living in an artificial environment in which you aren't exposed to many triggers. You may achieve sobriety in this setting without being prepared to deal with "real life" triggers like sitting on the couch where you used to drink or use. Recent research has indicated that outpatient treatment is as good as, or slightly better than, residential inpatient treatment because it extinguishes real life triggers. That's not to say that inpatient treatment is ineffective—it does work well for some people (*e.g.*, those addicts who cannot stay sober in an outpatient program)—but just realize that it is incomplete, that you are not even close to being "cured" once you leave the residential treatment facility. You still have a lot of work to do; you need follow-up treatment and counseling to help you overcome the many triggers you'll come in contact with when you leave the facility and return home.

Unfortunately, this information has not been widely disseminated, so most people still believe that inpatient treatment is the "gold standard" for addiction treatment.

Crushing the Cravings

Cravings are automatic brain responses that signal an association between a trigger and your substance of abuse. For a recovering addict, *any* alcohol or drug use—even prescription medication—tends to keep both triggers and cravings alive. This is why attempts at "controlled use" (*e.g.*, "I'll just do it now and then") do not work. Complete abstinence (no alcohol or drugs at all) is the surest and quickest way to "unlearn" the past association between triggers and your substance of abuse and effectively reduce cravings.

However, cravings will continue to arise, sometimes even years after you've been completely abstinent. They are a normal part of the recovery process. That's why it's absolutely necessary for you to develop some craving-crushing techniques you can utilize when the urge to use arises.

While cravings can sometimes feel irresistible, these techniques can help you ride out, resist, and crush many (if not all) of your cravings.

Craving-Crusher #1: Talking

Talk may be cheap, but it's one of the best ways to ride out a craving. When you get a craving, start talking about it right away with someone sober.

In your support group you'll learn how to discuss the experience of the craving, how it makes you feel, and what you think you should do about it. When a craving hits, immediately contact your sponsor, therapist, spouse/significant other, or someone else who knows what to say. It's important that the person you talk to understands that cravings are normal and that talking about it is very helpful in making it go away.

Craving-Crusher #2: Distracting Yourself

Cravings are self-limiting, physically generated events; they *will* go away on their own. If you can distract yourself, you may be able to ride them out. Distraction works because a craving is a physiologically generated response within the brain. If you can get your brain to concentrate on something else, the craving should disappear.

There are a variety of different ways to distract yourself; their effectiveness varies from person to person and situation to situation. A few ideas:

- doing a crossword puzzle
- exercising
- doing yoga
- meditating
- working out

- spending time on a hobby

- getting something to eat

- going for a walk

- going to the movies

- listening to music

Figure out which distractions work best for you. Then make a list, get your "supplies" together (pocket-sized crossword puzzles, iPod, walking shoes, CDs, etc.), and be ready.

Craving-Crusher #3: Using Flash Cards

This simple tool is a very effective way to crush cravings. On one side of the card you write the four most positive things that will occur if you stay sober; on the other side you write the four worst things that will occur if you use. For example:

Flash Card	
The Four Most Positive Things that will happen to me—if I stay sober:	The Four Worst Things that will happen to me—if I use or relapse:
1. I will be able to come home to see my wife and kids each evening.	1. I might go to jail if my probation is revoked when my drug screen is positive.
2. I can dig myself out of this financial mess by keeping my job.	2. I will not be able to see my kids anymore.
3. These cravings will eventually stop bothering me.	3. I will lose my job.
4. I will be a better role model for my children	4. I might drive drunk again, but this time kill someone.

Making the flash card is easy. Start with a separate piece of paper. On the paper, make a list of ten positive things that will happen if you resist the craving. Your list might include items such as:

If I Do Resist This Craving:

1. I'll be one step closer to complete sobriety.

2. I'll be able to have a clear-headed conversation with my spouse.

3. I'll be able to wake up without a headache.

4. I'll be able to show up at work on time and please my boss.

5. I'll be able to spend positive time with my family.

6. I'll be able to set a good example for my kids.

7. I'll be able to drive safely.

8. I'll be able to save money.

9. I'll be able to attend to my responsibilities at home.

10. I'll be able to eat full, nutritious meals.

On the same sheet of paper, jot down ten of the worst things that could happen if you give in to the craving. Your "use disaster" list could look something like this:

If I Don't Resist This Craving:

1. I might lose my job.

2. I might drive drunk and cause an accident.

3. I might cause further damage to my marriage.

4. I might endanger my kids.

5. I might ruin a friendship.

6. I might cause further damage to my health.

7. I might lose the respect of my family and friends.

8. I might lose my own self-respect.

9. I might neglect my responsibilities at home.

10. I might make my substance abuse problem even worse.

On a 3" x 5" index card, write "The Four Most Positive Things," then list your top four entries, in order, from your "If I *Do* Resist This Craving" list. On the other side, write "The Four Worst Things," then list your four worst entries, in order, from your "If I Don't Resist the Craving" list. Make copies of this card by hand (the more you write down the pros and cons, the more you will believe them) so you can keep one at work, one in your wallet, one in your car, one on your night stand, and so on in the places you're most likely to experience cravings. Look at these cards frequently to remind yourself of the benefits of continued sobriety as well as the consequences of drinking or using. When a craving does arise, reading both sides of your card will not only distract you, it will help to activate the logic systems in your cerebral cortex.

Since the consequences of using and abstaining will change over the course of your recovery, I strongly recommend that you make new flash cards once a week during the first twelve weeks of your treatment program (usually it is best to make them on Sunday evenings before the start of the week). This will keep your lists of positives and negatives about your sobriety and relapses current and help you stay focused on your priorities.

Craving-Crusher #4: Using Stress Management Techniques

While cravings often arise during periods of intense stress, even the normal stresses of everyday life can set them off. That's why learning new stress management techniques is vital for warding off future cravings and successfully managing those that do arise.

There are many effective stress management tools and techniques, including progressive deep muscle relaxation, yoga, meditation, deep breathing, and self-hypnosis. Hands-on methods of stress reduction such as massage, reflexology, acupressure, and acupuncture can also be very helpful. You can learn about these and other approaches from books, tapes, or the Internet, or attend classes at your local Y, health club, or community college. Ask your physician or therapist if he or she recommends any specific classes or teachers, and see if your health insurance offers discounts on classes or lists of recommended providers.

 For more information, see the stress management lesson on www.EnterHealth.com/HealingtheAddictedBrain.

Craving-Crusher #5: Visualizing

If you can visualize yourself resisting a craving, chances are you can turn that visualization into a reality. You can also use visualization to calm yourself when tension arises or to escape from situations that normally would incite addictive behaviors.

To do this, close your eyes and imagine, in great detail, a scene that is pleasant and includes information from all five of your senses. For example, you might visualize a tropical beach with warm, white sand, turquoise water and lapping waves, swaying palms, and the most comfortable hammock in the world tied between two trees. Smell the scent of the ocean, feel the warm breeze on your face, touch the soft padding on the hammock that awaits you, then climb in and lie back. Imagine the puffy clouds floating overhead, and just relax completely, listening to the sounds of the surf.

It's important to use all five senses in your visualization because that will engage a variety of areas in your brain and help to block out the craving more effectively. Practice calling this scene to mind when you are not having cravings. Then, when a craving begins to arise, take a break and go to that beautiful place in your mind.

What you visualize depends on you. Here are four categories of visualizations that are commonly effective for people working to overcome addictions:

1. *Relaxing scenario*—This is the type of visualization described above. Just picturing yourself in peaceful surroundings—some people call this their "happy place"—can be very relaxing, distracting, and stress-reducing.

2. *Positive scenario*—You might picture yourself remaining sober and taking your children to the park, doing really excellent work, or having the perfect romantic date with your spouse or significant other.

3. *Negative scenario*—One of my patients imagined shooting IV heroin at his grandmother's house, passing out with the needle in his arm, and his grandmother discovering him, having a heart attack, and dying on top of him. He practiced this very negative visualization several times and said that when he had cravings, this scenario would give him the strength to completely obliterate them.

4. *Conquering scenario*—Because cravings have a time limit, you may find it helpful to visualize the craving as a wave that eventually flattens out and disappears. Picture yourself as a master surfer on a surfboard, riding the wave in to shore, waiting for it to melt away. Or you may want to visualize the craving as being the "bad guy" in a video game with you playing the part of the "good guy," blasting away and eventually killing it.

You're not limited to these four categories of visualizations. If another scenario works for you, use it. The important thing is to develop your visualizations and practice imagining them now, before cravings arise.

You can learn about visualization from books, tapes, and the Internet. Your therapist, sponsor, or other people in your groups may also be able to teach you how to visualize.

To learn more about visualization, go to www.EnterHealth.com/ HealingtheAddictedBrain.

Key Ways to Control Your Cravings

Your addiction changed your life for the worse; now you must begin to change it for the better. When you make key pro-recovery changes, you will immediately decrease the frequency and power of your future cravings.

Always remember that you *can* control your cravings by reducing your exposure to triggers as much as possible and by responding to harmful desires that do arise. Keep this little diagram in mind:

Trigger → Thought → Craving

Many people mistakenly believe that this terrible progression is inevitable. *You may not be able to completely eliminate your exposure to triggers, but you always have control over your thoughts.* (See Chapter 2.) It can be difficult to replace pro-addiction thoughts with thoughts of staying sober and the benefits that come from remaining sober, but it can be done.

Keep working on specific techniques for replacing pro-addiction thoughts with pro-recovery thoughts, and remember these general principles:

- Remain committed to living a clean, alcohol- and drug-free life.
- Change your lifestyle by developing new friends and activities.
- Be patient.
- Be persistent.
- Be careful.
- Do not give in to temptation, as *any* alcohol or drug use will strengthen cravings.
- Use positive behavior.

• Avoid unhealthy situations; do not test yourself.

• Say yes to new sober friends and new sober activities.

Remember, cravings are common in the recovery process. They are *not* a sign of weakness or failure. Cravings are like waves in the ocean: they may come in big and strong, but they go out with no strength at all.

Key Points Review

- A trigger is any idea, concept, person, place, thing, or emotional state that stimulates the destructive thinking that arouses the urge (craving) to drink or use.

- When you drink or use, your brain remembers the high or euphoria you experienced and links these very positive feelings to the people, places, items, thoughts, or emotions related to drinking or using.

- The first step in controlling your triggers is to identify them.

- Charting triggers and keeping a daily record of them can help you understand how those triggers work.

- You can help control your cravings by avoiding your triggers whenever possible.

- Because you can't always avoid all of your triggers, you must learn to control your reactions to them.

- You can weaken your cravings by continually resisting the urge to drink or use when exposed to triggers.

- Complete abstinence is the surest way to "unlearn" the past association between triggers and your substance of abuse and effectively reduce cravings.

- People in recovery typically give in to only about 5 percent of their cravings. This means that right now you can resist almost all (95 percent) of your cravings.

- Talking, distracting yourself, using flash cards, stress management techniques, and visualization are all effective ways to resist, ride out, and crush cravings.

- There are many safe, nonaddicting medications that can help reduce cravings.

- Cravings are natural and unavoidable, but you do *not* have to give in to them.

CHAPTER FOUR

Medications to Initiate Recovery and Help Maintain Sobriety

Traditionally, physicians have not had much in their little black bags to offer to their patients struggling to remain sober. There is Antabuse, a medicine that works by literally making you sick when you drink alcohol, and naltrexone, which acts in the brain to prevent alcohol or opiates from making you drunk or high. Antabuse performs exactly as described, but alcoholics loathe taking it, due to its unpleasant actions. And while naltrexone is effective, it must be taken every day, or its effects soon wear off. Countless addicts taking naltrexone while in recovery convince themselves that they must be cured because they can now drink or use without getting high. So they stop taking their medicine. Then, of course, there is methadone for opiate addicts. This medicine has saved a lot of lives but can be very difficult to obtain, due to social attitudes and legal hurdles.

Antabuse, naltrexone, and methadone are good medicines, albeit with limited effectiveness and practicality. Fortunately, new scientific advances have made possible a new generation of anti-addiction medications that offer unprecedented possibilities for treatment and recovery. Newly approved medications and treatment protocols make it possible for people to stay on their "no high" medicines, reduce their cravings, and help rebalance the brain's biochemistry.

Let's examine the latest medicines that help people maintain their so-briety, then review some of the medications used to help ease withdrawal from alcohol and various substances.

Connecting with the Receptors

As you read through this chapter, keep these three definitions in mind:

- *Agonist*—something that binds to a cell receptor and triggers a response. An agonist is like a key that fits into the lock to open the door. Morphine is an agonist that fits into opiate receptors to trigger the high.

- *Antagonist*—something that binds to a cell receptor but does not trigger the response, or only does so weakly. In one sense, an antagonist is like bubble gum in a door lock; it can't unlock the door, but it prevents the key from being put in, so the door remains shut. As you'll see below, the medicines naloxone/nal-trexone are antagonists that fit into certain receptors and pre-vents the morphine from attaching.

- *Mixed agonist/antagonist*—a substance that behaves like ei-ther an agonist or antagonist, depending on the dosage, it can change its actions on the receptor.

Anti-Addiction Medicines for Alcoholism

Treatment of alcohol addiction has recently been greatly enhanced thanks to two new medications, Vivitrol and Campral. Vivitrol encourages the addict to cut back on alcohol intake, thereby reducing or eliminating ongoing brain damage, while Campral helps accelerate repairs to brain systems. With less poison coming in and repairs occurring at a faster rate, the brain is better able to accept new, healthy thinking patterns and master sober life skills. Either individually or in combination, Vivitrol and Campral are the new hope millions of alcoholics have been waiting for. Let's take a closer look at these two medicines, how they work, and how they're used.

Vivitrol—Blocking the High

Vivitrol is a new formulation of a well-known treatment for both opiate and alcohol addiction that's been used for many years. It's more than a repackaging, however, for Vivitrol is a safe, effective, injectable, and long-lasting means of controlling cravings and nearly eliminating the "slips" and relapses that were so common with earlier medications. For these and other reasons, Vivitrol is the breakthrough medicine that will revolutionize the treatment of alcoholism.

The active ingredient in Vivitrol is naltrexone, an opiate antagonist used to treat both alcohol and opiate dependence. Naltrexone works by "plugging in" to opioid receptors found on certain brain cells, thus preventing alcohol (or opiate) molecules from doing the same thing. In effect, naltrexone crowds out alcohol molecules, getting there first and "jamming the lock." Unable to connect with these brain receptors, the alcohol/opiate molecules cannot activate pleasure pathways in the brain and therefore cannot trigger a high. The alcohol/opiate molecules can still plug into other brain cells to cause slurred speech, drowsiness, and other symptoms of being intoxicated, but they are locked out of the cells that trigger a high. This means that while you're on naltrexone, you can experience all the unpleasant effects of being drunk, but not the "good" one, not the high that alcoholics/opiate addicts crave.

When I was principal investigator on one of the national Vivitrol research trials, a forty-seven-year-old prominent female judge named Yvonne became one of our research patients. Yvonne desperately wanted to give up the quart of bourbon she typically drank every night, for her husband had just filed for separation and taken their two daughters. He gave his wife an ultimatum: get help, or he would file for divorce. After a seven-day withdrawal stabilization to get her off the bourbon safely, Yvonne was given her first Vivitrol injection. Within two weeks, she noted that her cravings had all but disappeared. She began attending AA, got a sponsor, and after she had been sober for a month, her husband and daughters returned to live with her. After about six weeks on Vivitrol—following her second injection—she had a particularly hard day on the bench and at home with one of her daughters. So she snuck out to a bar she used to visit on the way home and started drinking bourbon. But about halfway through her first drink she felt full and did not want to drink anymore. Yvonne set down the drink, called her sponsor to talk about what she had done, and went to an AA meeting that night. She later told her therapist that when she was in the bar, she was quite angry that she could not get drunk, could not get the "relief" that she wanted from her bourbon. Later, of course, she was greatly relieved that she had had only a half a serving, rather than the entire quart she was accustomed to drinking.

Naltrexone in the pill form was approved by the FDA for use in treating alcohol addiction in 1994 and opiate addiction in the 1970s, so we have almost four decade's worth of experience with the medicine. Its primary weakness is that it must be taken every single day or its effects will wear off in a few days. People in recovery often forget, or deliberately neglect, to take their daily pills. "Unprotected" by their medicine, they drink or use again, feel the euphoria, and fall into a lapse or relapse. (In fact, naltrexone's very effectiveness makes it easy for addicts to convince themselves that they can handle their alcohol and that therefore they are cured.) Family members, physicians, counselors, and friends often nag, plead, prod, and threaten addicts, trying to get them to take the medicine again, usually to no avail.

Vivitrol eliminates this major weakness (noncompliance) because it is a long-lasting, injectable version of naltrexone administered just once a month at the doctor's office. A major technical breakthrough was needed to convert relatively short-acting naltrexone pills into a long-lasting injectable version, and that breakthrough came in the form of biodegradable molecules called microspheres. A shot of Vivitrol injects the microscopic spheres into the buttocks, and from there they slowly and methodically migrate into the bloodstream. As the individual spheres break down over the course of thirty days, they release a continual stream of naltrexone into the blood. The alcoholic does not have to remember—and cannot deliberately "forget"—to take the medicine. For a full month there is almost no chance of getting drunk (feeling high/eupohoric), and no need for nagging.

Vivitrol also has a significant psychological advantage: the fact that it's "a shot the doc gives" makes it easier to accept it as a medicine that treats a chronic medical illness. Rather than being a punishment for sinful behavior, it's just a shot for a disease, like an insulin injection for diabetes. By allowing us to view addiction as a disease, Vivitrol will help remove the terrible stigma society attaches to alcoholism/drug addiction—a misguided moral judgment that prevents most from receiving proper treatment.

The fact that it's long-lasting and psychologically acceptable, as well as safe and effective, helps overcome the compliance issue; it's much easier to get people to stay with injectable Vivitrol monthly than it is to get them to swallow daily naltrexone pills.

Let's take a closer look at what Vivitrol does, and how you use it to overcome your urge to use alcohol/opiates.

Vivitrol's Practical Application

By binding to and blocking certain neuroreceptors in your brain, Vivitrol does three things:

- It decreases your urge to use alcohol (or opiates) by up to 90 percent compared to those not using the medication. This is the same tremendous result we typically see with oral naltrexone, a phenomenal improvement. Since you don't "crave" alcohol/opiates, you're much less likely to drink or use.

- If you do drink or use, Vivitrol blocks the euphoria or the high you normally get. This means that most people cannot get the "drunk" feeling while they are on Vivitrol. You can have all of the unpleasant symptoms of intoxication, such as driving or walking poorly, but none of the pleasant effects—a very frustrating situation that serves as an inducement to stop drinking or using.

• By blocking the high, Vivitrol prevents the first drink from becoming the first of several. Many people only plan to have a single beer, for example, but the pleasurable buzz they get encourages them to continue drinking. The one beer becomes three, ten, or even twenty-four—a full case! With Vivitrol you don't get the pleasurable sensations from the first beer, so you have no incentive to continue drinking. Instead, you are more likely to realize you slipped and to call your sponsor.

Thanks to these actions, Vivitrol reduced the median number of "drinking days" per month from 15.2 to 0.2 in a recent study.

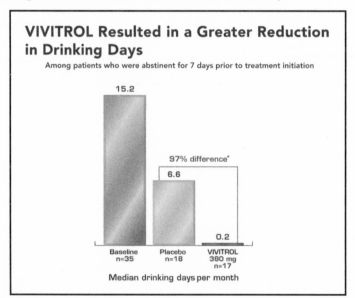

You Can Still Have Fun!

Some patients fear that since Vivitrol interferes with the dopamine system and other parts of the brain responsible for pleasure, it will "dull them out." They worry that while they're on Vivitrol, they will be unable to feel the joy one gets from a job well done, receiving a good grade at school, seeing a great concert, and so on. Fortunately, that does not happen. There are many ways to stimulate the brain's pleasure centers; Vivitrol only interferes with the alcohol/opiate-induced high. You can continue to enjoy life's many pleasures while on the medicine.

How It's Administered

Three hundred and eighty milligrams of Vivitrol are injected by your doctor/nurse into the buttocks once a month, alternating sides each month.

Time It Takes to Produce Effects

Vivitrol works quickly, usually within two to three days.

Side Effects

Vivitrol is safe, well-tolerated and nonaddicting. Its primary side effect is nausea, which, if it occurs at all, will usually only appear two to four days after the first injection. Nausea is not usually an issue after the first injection. Occasionally, patients will have a headache, feeling of sedation, or some tenderness at the injection site for a short time after receiving the shot. These symptoms are mild in most cases and, in any case, are infinitely less troublesome than the side effects of alcohol/opiates.

One of the reasons for the lack of side effects is that the dose of Vivitrol given with each injection is relatively small: 380 mg/month. Medicines taken by mouth are transported from the intestines to the liver, where enzymes metabolize and deactivate some portion of them. But Vivitrol is injected into the muscle, then released into the bloodstream, which means it does not go right to the liver, where some of it would be destroyed. The medicine is eventually broken down within the body, but since it skips the first trip to the liver, more is available for use, and a smaller dose will suffice.

The normal daily dose of oral naltrexone is 50 mg, which adds up to about 1,500 mg per month. At that level, naltrexone is safe and well-tolerated. With a monthly injection of Vivitrol, you're only getting 380 mg of naltrexone, about 70 percent less than a month's dosage of pills—but much more (approximately four times more) of it is available and active in the brain because it bypasses the first trip to the liver. This smaller but equally effective dose is well within the safe range and may account for the minimal side effects most patients experience.

Both Vivitrol and naltrexone come with a "black box warning," a package label containing a strong warning of potential side effects, required by the FDA. This black box warning suggests you might develop significant liver problems if you use Vivitrol or naltrexone for a long period of time without having a doctor monitor your blood and liver tests. That sounds alarming, but the warning is based on a single study performed on non-addicted obese people who were taking six times the normal daily dose of naltrexone (300 mg). Simply being obese places a large "fat load" on the liver, and adding six times the normal dose of naltrexone is asking for trouble—which occurred, for some of the participants had abnormal liver tests. It's a stretch to conclude that therefore Vivitrol is dangerous, but it's a good idea for your physician to check your blood liver tests four times a year, just to be sure. Remember that alcohol is much more toxic to your liver.

Vivitrol does not interact with other medications very much, so it can be added to just about any current medication regimen without concern. However, you should tell your physician about all of the medication you are taking before starting on Vivitrol. There are two medicines that definitely *cannot* be taken simultaneously with Vivitrol: Suboxone and methadone. Taking Vivitrol with either of these two will cause opiate withdrawal.

Special Benefit: Vivitrol's Positive Impact on the Family

Vivitrol can have a powerful and positive influence on your family or support system. They have lived with the stress, fear, chaos, and uncertainty of addiction for years, wondering what you will do next, whether you'll disappoint the children again, spend all the family's money, be found face down in a gutter, and so on. Once you start taking Vivitrol, they'll see that you're not getting drunk or high anymore, that you don't even have many urges to do so. They'll see that even when you do take a drink, you tend to stop with one. When they realize that you will not lapse for at least thirty days after each injection, they'll begin to feel that they can finally start to their lives in order.

Family and other members of your support system will become determined allies of your doctor, encouraging you to make your follow-up Vivitrol injection appointments and to stick with the other parts of your recovery program. Excited by the possibility of success, they will be more willing than ever to participate in family support groups and learn the new skills that will help them help you remain sober. All of a sudden, trust starts to begin to return to the family system.

 For more information on Vivitrol, please see www.EnterHealth. com/HealingtheAddictedBrain.

Campral—Repairing the Brain

Thirty-year-old Jeri had already been through two residential alcohol treatment programs and one outpatient program when she came to my institute in Dallas, hoping that the new medicine she had heard about would help her. As I spoke with her, I could tell that she was eager to get sober but had difficulty paying attention, understanding, and retaining new information. As she put it, "When they tell me something in the programs, it makes sense, and I want to do it, but it just doesn't stick. And then it's too hard to put what they tell me into practice in real life, outside of the treatment centers." As part of her overall treatment program, we put her on Campral (the new medicine she had heard about). Eight weeks later she said, "I finally get what they're telling me. I mean, I can pay attention and get it!" Soon Jeri had mastered many of the techniques that she needed to stay sober, was attending AA regularly, and said that her cravings for alcohol had all but disappeared.

Campral (generic name acamprosate) represents an exciting new advance in alcohol treatment because we think it helps the brain heal.

Vivitrol prevents you from getting drunk or high when you drink or use opiates, which means you'll put a lot less of these poisonous substances into your body and give your brain a chance to begin to recover. Unfortunately, the healing process can take months or even years, a frustratingly long period of time during which you'll continue to wrestle with memory and thinking difficulties and struggle to master healthy coping skills. Until the new skills are mastered, the risk of relapse will be ever present.

Speeding the brain's recovery process reduces the risk of relapse, and that's what we think Campral does. By rebalancing certain neurotransmitter systems deep within the brain, Campral can improve the alcoholic's cognitive skills and ability to learn new coping skills, lessen the cravings for alcohol and the odds of relapse even more, and accelerate the recovery process.

Let's take a closer look at Campral's actions and at how you use it to restore the brain to health.

Campral's Practical Application

Campral has been used in Europe since the late 1980s to reduce alcohol cravings in problem drinkers. In 2004, the Food and Drug Administration approved the medication for the treatment of alcohol dependence in the United States.

Remember that addiction damages both the cortex and the limbic region of the brain. Talking therapy helps to deal with problems governed by the cortex, but it cannot reach deep within the brain to the limbic region. We think Campral can. By helping to rebalance certain neurotransmitter systems, this medicine can help repair damaged systems in the limbic region. This repair can reduce cravings and makes it easier for the brain to concentrate on cortex-based talking therapy.

Although Campral's precise mechanism of action is not known, it appears to restore the balance in certain neurotransmitter pathways—most likely the GABA and glutamate systems—that have been altered by chronic alcohol consumption.

The GABA neurotransmitter system is responsible for keeping you calm and relaxed. The glutamate neurotransmitter system does just the opposite, energizing and revving you up. The two systems have opposite actions, like the gas pedal and brake in a car. The two are equally important and must be equally "strong"; otherwise you would be out of balance, always either revved up or going too slow.

Drinking alcohol stimulates the GABA system—the brain's "brake pedal"—making you feel relaxed and sedated. At the same time, alcohol suppresses the glutamate system. It's as if the brake is being pushed and the accelerator is not. When the alcohol wears off, the excitatory glutamate system "rebounds." Now it's as if someone has taken their foot off your brain's brake and is stepping on the gas pedal; you feel more irritable and agitated, and you may have difficulty sleeping.

Heavy drinkers develop tolerance to alcohol, which modifies the GABA system further and means that you need larger and larger doses of alcohol to "put on the brakes," to stimulate the GABA system enough that you slow down and relax. Heavy use of alcohol also damages the glutamate system, "turbocharging" it so that your internal accelerator is "pressed to the floor" when the alcohol wears off. In effect, heavy alcohol use throws the entire system out of whack by "wearing out the brakes" and "stomping on the accelerator." This can trigger elevated blood pressure, rapid heart rate, irritability, difficulty concentrating, difficulty sleeping, and other problems.

Campral appears to restore the normal balance between the GABA and glutamate systems. We're not sure exactly how it does so, but patients report that after taking this medicine for six to eight weeks, they begin to feel calmer, handle stress more effectively, concentrate and focus better, and have fewer cravings for alcohol.

How It's Administered

Campral is not well absorbed by the gastrointestinal tract: only about 10 percent of what you take passes into the body. You need about 200 mg of Campral per day into your bloodstream to rebalance your GABA and glutamate systems, which means you have to take about 2000 mg Campral per day—the amount found in six tablets. Rather than swallow all six at once, people usually take two tablets three times a day. But it can be difficult to remember the middle dose, so I usually begin by prescribing two tablets three times a day for the first two weeks, then have my patients switch to three tablets twice a day. This eliminates the middle (lunch) dose and helps improve compliance. Patients usually take Campral for at least a year. After that, you and your physician can consider discontinuing it.

Side Effects

Campral is nontoxic and nonaddicting. Side effects are minimal, the main one being diarrhea. Fortunately, this side effect is quite infrequent, especially after the first couple of days of being on the medicine. Other even less common side effects include nausea, itching, and intestinal gas. Campral usually does not interact with other medications, so it can be added to just about any medication regimen without concern, based on your physician's recommendation. However, it is vital that you give your physician a full list of all medicines you are taking.

 For more information on Campral, please see www.EnterHealth. com/HealingtheAddictedBrain.

Other Medicines for Alcoholism

Naturally, some alcoholics do not respond to Vivitrol or Campral in terms of experiencing a physiological benefit (decreased cravings, etc.). In these cases, I might use other medications, including Antabuse and Topomax:

these have their uses but are considered "second-line," meaning that they are generally only tried after other medicines have not been successful.

- *Disulfiram (trade name Antabuse)*—An old treatment for alcoholism, disulfiram was approved by the FDA for this use back in 1951. Disulfiram is a sensitizing agent that triggers a highly unpleasant reaction when you drink even a small amount of alcohol. It does so by interfering with the metabolic processes that break down alcohol, resulting in an accumulation of acetaldehyde in the blood. This toxic by-product of normal alcohol metabolism produces a complex of highly unpleasant symptoms, including intense nausea and vomiting, sweating, flushed skin, a throbbing headache, respiratory difficulties, blurred vision, and confusion. In fact, if an alcoholic drinks alcohol while they are taking disulfiram, they should be taken to the ER just to be safe during the acute toxicity reaction. Disulfiram acts only as a deterrent; it does not interfere with alcohol's ability to trigger a high, and it does not heal any of the damage caused by the alcoholism. This medication is effective and can be an integral part of certain recovery programs. However, the toxic reaction disulfiram triggers raises some safety issues; as a result, it is not usually used as a first-line treatment for alcoholism by primary care physicians (such as family practitioners and internists). Instead it may be used by addiction treatment specialists along with Vivitrol, or Vivitrol plus Campral, or used by itself if other standard treatments fail. The standard dose of disulfiram is 250 mg per day. Your doctor should perform blood tests every quarter to check for elevated liver enzymes.

 For more information on Antabuse, please see www.Enter-Health.com/HealingtheAddictedBrain.

- *Topirimate (trade name Topomax)*—Topirimate is an anticonvulsant mood-stabilizing medication. It has not yet been approved by the FDA for the treatment of alcoholism, although physicians are allowed to use it for that purpose. In several scientific studies, topirimate helped reduce alcohol cravings and make withdrawal easier. The medicine may reduce cravings by lowering brain levels of the neurotransmitter dopamine, which is believed to create the pleasurable sensations alcoholics get from drinking. Topirimate also seems to reduce anxiety and potentially resets the brain's chemistry. Unfortunately, the medicine has a number of unpleasant side effects and should only be administered by an addiction treatment specialist.

• *Nalmefene (trade name Revex), ondansetron (trade name Zofran), and baclofen (trade name Lioresal)*—These three medicines have been studied and show some promise for reducing alcohol cravings and intake. They may have a role to play in some specific treatment protocols, but they don't compare in effectiveness to Vivitrol and Campral at this time.

Anti-Addiction Medicines for Opiates/Opioids

Technically speaking, the word "opiate" means a derivative of the opium poppy, such as morphine and codeine, while "opioid" refers to both opiates and a wide range of synthetic compounds. However, many people use "opiate" to refer to both opiates and opioids. Commonly used opiates include heroin, morphine, methadone, codeine, fentanyl, hydromorphone, Demerol (generic name meperidine), OxyContin (generic name oxycodone), and Lortab (generic name hydrocodone).

Various medications had been proposed as treatments for opiate addiction, but by the early 1960s the medical profession concluded that no known treatment could permanently help more than a small fraction of long-term opiate addicts, 70 to 90 percent of whom would relapse within a short time.

We *do* have an effective medicine: the synthetic narcotic called methadone. Developed in the 1930s, methadone is inexpensive and long lasting, with a single dose sufficing for an entire day. When properly used, methadone effectively stabilizes opioid addicts without producing any of the euphoria or tolerance seen with opiates. While methadone is subject to producing a high when used in large doses and has the possibility of being abused, overall, it is an excellent treatment option. Unfortunately, methadone maintenance treatment remains a controversial issue among public officials, the medical profession, and the public at large. Negative attitudes based on inaccurate education about methadone, along with a confusing tangle of regulations surrounding its use, make it difficult for most opiate addicts to use methadone as a treatment option. As a result, as recently as 2005, 75 percent of all opiate addicts were not receiving treatment, even though an effective medicine exists.

Suboxone, a Revolutionary Approach to Opioid Addiction Treatment

In 2002, the FDA approved a new medicine for use in treating opioid dependence. This was buprenorphine, a "partial-agonist" opioid that in low doses mimics the effects of opioid agonists such as heroin and oxycodone, and in higher doses mimics the effects of the opiate antagonist naltrexone. It does this by binding tightly to opiate receptors in the brain, sitting there like a weak agonist and removing the craving but not producing a high. It acts like a piece of gum in a lock, shutting out the real opiates when they try to bind to the receptors and trigger a high. They can't get in, so there's no high.

Narcotic addicts are commonly prescribed buprenorphine in the form of the medicine called Suboxone, which contains buprenorphine and naloxone. Suboxone is used as a first-line treatment for opiate addiction to reduce illegal opioid use and to help patients stay in treatment by blocking the effects of opioids, decreasing cravings, and suppressing any major symptoms of withdrawal. Most narcotic addicts seem to benefit from Suboxone regardless of which opiates they were using, or for how long.

Ben's story was typical for an opiate addict. Twenty-nine years old when he came to my institute seeking help for heroin addiction, he said that he just hated his life on opiates and detested being captive to his addiction. If he missed the timing of his "hit" by two hours, he began to feel sick (the early symptoms of opiate withdrawal) and his cravings would "go through the roof," so he always had to make sure that he had his supply available, no matter where he was or what he was doing. "For the last couple of years," he said, "I haven't really felt the rush when I use. I only do it so I won't get sick or go crazy. That's why I hate my life." Fortunately, within a week of starting on Suboxone he was a completely changed person. He told me that this was the first time that he had felt normal since he was sixteen.

Suboxone is a major advance in the treatment of opiate addiction because it blocks the effects of opiates in the brain. If you slip and use while you're on the drug, you don't get the high. Deprived of the "benefit" of using, you're less likely to relapse. With no cravings or desire to use, patients can participate very successfully in an outpatient treatment and 12-step program to learn the coping skills needed to maintain a sober lifestyle going forward.

Just as Vivitrol and Campral are revolutionizing the treatment of alcohol addiction, Suboxone is an amazingly effective tool to treat opiate addiction when it is used as part of a comprehensive treatment program.

How It's Administered

Suboxone should not be started until the patient is in withdrawal, for if there are still opiates in his or her system when the Suboxone is given, the drug will behave like an antagonist, blocking the effects of the opiates and throwing the patient into an uncomfortable withdrawal state. The dosage is typically adjusted during the first couple days of usage. As soon as the optimal dosage is found, the patient will feel comfortable and have almost no cravings.

Although it varies from case to case, most patients need to be on Suboxone at least nine to twelve months before their systems are stabilized and then, with the help of their physicians, many of them can taper off slowly. After they are completely off Suboxone for two weeks, it's generally best to use Vivitrol for at least another one to two years to continue blocking the possibility of getting high from opiates during a relapse.

Side Effects

Potential side effects include sweating, headache, pain, nausea, constipation, and trouble sleeping. It can also lead to opiate withdrawal symptoms if its use is stopped suddenly.

 For more information on Suboxone, please see www.Enter Health.com/HealingtheAddictedBrain.

Since late 2010, we have yet another great choice to treat opiate addiction –Vivitrol. Yes, the same medication I discussed as the primary treatment for alcohol dependence is now FDA-approved to prevent relapse for opiate addicts. (Please see the previous Vivitrol discussion for more detailed information.) This new indication for Vivitrol is not that surprising because Naltrexone, the active ingredient in Vivitrol, has been approved to treat opiate addiction since the 1960s, and, fortunately, it has the same three beneficial effects for these patients as it does for alcoholics: significantly decreases urges to use (cravings), blocks the high or euphoria from opiate use, and decreases the severity of a relapse. Yet, just like in alcoholism, Vivitrol also addresses the compliance issue for opiate addicts – it only needs to be injected once every 30 days, and it lasts all month. So how does the same medication work so effectively to treat both alcoholism and opiate addiction? Well, the real answer is we do not actually know how it does it, but in the future I believe we will find an injured common pathway in the addicted brains, of both alcoholics and opiate addicts.

In regards to actual use, unlike in alcoholism where you only need to wait four days after your last drink to receive Vivitrol, opiate addicts need to wait seven to ten days after their last use to get their first injection (or fourteen days after their last suboxone dose). Otherwise, Vivitrol can set off opiate withdrawal. As always, Vivitrol needs to be used in partnership with other parts of a comprehensive treatment program.

So now we have a choice between Suboxone or Vivitrol to treat opiate addiction. In my opinion, for most opiate addicts I would start with

Suboxone for nine to twelve months then transition to Vivitrol for one to two years. However, some opiate addicts will start Vivitrol seven to ten days after their last use and never use Suboxone. It really depends on the individual patient's circumstances. We need more research to determine the absolute best protocol, but at least we have two effective choices.

Anti-Addiction Medicines for Stimulants

Stimulants such as cocaine and various amphetamines (especially methamphetamine, certain designer drugs like MDMA and bath salts) are popular drugs of abuse; their users span the entire spectrum of social and economic classes. People as young as twelve and as old as seventy-five can find themselves hooked on cocaine in its various forms, or on methamphetamine. Repeated use of stimulants may significantly alter the balance of chemicals in your brain, affecting your mood, sleep, energy level, and most importantly your thinking ability. These brain chemical imbalances caused by stimulant addiction can cause severe cravings during the early sobriety period (up to twelve to eighteen months after stopping the stimulant) and both these severe cravings for the stimulant as well as the trouble thinking clearly can cause a high risk of relapse to stimulant or other drug use. Science has made significant progress on developing new forms of talking therapy treatments for stimulant addiction, such as Voucher-based therapy, where stimulant addicts who reach specific therapy and abstinence goals, receive a voucher which they can use for food or other useful products. However, even with these new psychosocial treatment findings, stimulant addicts' treatment drop-out rates remain at over 50 percent.

Unfortunately, no medications have been specifically approved for the treatment of stimulant dependence by the FDA at this time. However a variety of medications for stimulant addiction have been tested in numerous research trials sponsored by the National Institutes of Health, yet so far none have generated a great deal of excitement among addiction treatment specialists. One medicine, modafinil (trade name Provigil), which is used to treat sleep disorders, does show real promise as an oral medicine for cocaine addiction, possibly by reducing symptoms of cocaine withdrawal. In a recent double-blind, placebo-controlled study, this medicine, at a dose of 200mg per day, in combination with talking therapy increased the ability of some addicts to abstain from using cocaine, as well as reducing their cravings. Another medication propranolol (trade name Inderal) seems to also help decrease the symptoms of cocaine withdrawal. These first two potential medications seem to help reduce the withdrawal symptoms from cocaine addiction. Yet another group of potential "anti-stimulant" medications have been found to actually help to prevent relapse to stimulant use (especially cocaine) during the later phases of treatment. Some of the more promising medications used for this goal include topiramate, (trade name Topamax) disulfiram (trade name Antabuse), gabapentin (trade name Neurontin) and baclofen (trade name Lioresal). Research scientists are even evaluating a new vaccine (given by injection) that works by using antibodies against cocaine to prevent it from gaining access to the brain.

In general, the similarities between the ways that the major stimulants, cocaine and methamphetamine, effect the brain, allow the above medications to help treat both classes of stimulants. However, specifically the medication buproprion (trade name Wellbutrin) has shown some good clinical evidence that it can help reduce relapse in Methamphetamine addicts, even though it does not appear to work with cocaine addicts.

Anti-Addiction Medicines for Sedatives

The prescription medicines known as benzodiazepines and barbiturates have sedating effects. The benzodiazepines—including Valium (generic name diazepam), Xanax (generic name alprazolam), Klonopin (generic name clonazepam), and Restoril (generic name temazepam)—are mild sedatives, while the barbiturates—including phenobarbital, pentobarbital, and secobarbital—are major tranquilizers. Like alcohol, these medications are frequently abused for their calming effects and can produce a high in some patients.

There are no medications approved by the FDA specifically to treat sedative addiction. However, certain medicines can be used to help sedative abusers with the anxiety they often struggle with after they have gone through withdrawal (often a great deal more anxiety than other types of addicts face). Many sedative abusers began using these drugs to relieve an anxiety disorder. With the drugs removed, their original anxiety returns full-blown—and possibly stronger than ever—but they can no longer turn to the medicines they abused for help. Sedative abusers also seem to have significant problems with insomnia, especially early in sobriety.

Fortunately, there are nonaddicting medications that can treat anxiety or insomnia once the withdrawal stabilization process is complete. These include antiseizure/antiepileptic medicines, atypical antipsychotics, and antidepressants.

- *Antiseizure/antiepileptic medications*—These medications, approved by the FDA to treat patients with ongoing seizures, are very effective at decreasing anxiety. They are hypothesized to work at GABA receptors and elsewhere in the brain to calm you down, reduce anxiety, and increase the ability to sleep. Neurontin (generic name gabapentin) and Trileptal (generic name oxcarbazepine) are among the medicines that help relieve anxiety in a nonaddicting manner. (In many cases these medicines also have antidepressant, antimania, and pain-relieving effects. Therefore, they can be helpful for sedative addicts who began abusing drugs to help with their underlying depression, mania, and pain.)

- *Atypical antipsychotic medications*—This class of medications is used to treat schizophrenia and, to a lesser degree, bipolar disorder. Low doses of these medications—including Seroquel (generic name quetiapine) and Risperdal (generic name risperidone)— are also helpful in relieving anxiety and appear to have some antidepressant properties.

- *Antidepressant medications*—Lexapro (generic name escitalopram), Zoloft (generic name sertraline), Effexor XR (generic name venlafaxine),

Pristiq (generic name desvenlafaxine), and other antidepressants are often very effective at reducing anxiety. They can also help with any coexisting depression sedative abusers may suffer from.

Depending on individual needs, these medicines may be used alone or in various combinations. Medications in all three of these classes are nonaddicting and do not produce euphoria, which means they cannot be abused and can be used on an ongoing basis by people with sedative addiction issues. Vistaril (generic name Hydroxyzine), an antihistamine, is even another good choice to manage anxiety.

Remember, however, that medicine by itself is not enough. The most effective approach to treating anxiety includes nonaddicting medications, psychotherapy, and appropriate stress management techniques such as yoga, meditation, and deep breathing exercises.

Anti-Addiction Medicines for Hallucinogens

Drugs of many classes can produce hallucinations. The most commonly abused hallucinogens include marijuana, LSD (lysergic acid diethylamide), mescaline, PCP (phencyclidine piperidine), and designer drugs such as MDMA ("ecstasy," which is also a stimulant).

Treatments for Marijuana Dependence

Most people think marijuana is perfectly safe and nonaddictive, but that could not be further from the truth, because it does have strong addictive potential, just like any other drug that causes euphoria.

One of the reasons that people believe marijuana is nonaddictive is that they don't see any withdrawal symptoms when they stop smoking it. There actually *are* withdrawal symptoms but they take some time to manifest, and by then the user doesn't link the symptoms to the marijuana use. Marijuana smoke contains some 250 different chemical components. One of these is THC (delta-9-tetrahydrocannibinol), a primary active ingredient triggering marijuana's effects. THC easily moves into the bloodstream and then into the fat cells, where it remains for a long time after you stop smoking marijuana. (Forty-two days can pass between the time you stop smoking marijuana and the time the THC is finally removed from all the fat cells in your body.) This means that, in effect, marijuana's effects last a long time and withdrawal symptoms do not usually appear for two or three weeks after you stop smoking it, when the THC is in the process of being removed. This time lag makes it difficult to identify the insomnia, irritability, agitation, anxiety, and cravings that finally do appear as marijuana withdrawal symptoms. Instead, you simply feel like lighting up again.

There are no medicines approved specifically to treat marijuana dependence. However, I have had success with a medicine called Seroquel (generic name quetiapine). Seroquel is an antipsychotic medication used to treat schizophrenia and, to a lesser degree, bipolar disorder. In low doses, it is also a very effective antianxiety and anticraving medication. I sometimes encourage my patients to use a pill cutter to quarter a 25 mg dose tablet of Seroquel, giving them four pills of approximately 6.25 mg each. These small doses can be very effective in treating marijuana cravings.

Along with Seroquel, I have also recommended Lexapro, Zoloft, and other SSRI antidepressants. In addition to reducing anxiety, they can also treat any ongoing problems with depression that may arise when the marijuana has been withdrawn. Unfortunately, at this time we have no specific pharmacological treatments for addiction to any of the other hallucinogens, but hopefully that will change as new research findings come to light.

New and Old Anti-Addiction Medicines Combine to Offer Hope

The "old" medicines for addiction were helpful but limited, for they did not repair damage to the brain, and people in recovery often forgot to take them, or deliberately tossed them aside. Thanks to recent scientific breakthroughs, we can now offer people a long-lasting medicine that need be administered only once a month, another that helps repair brain damage, and still others that help reduce cravings and encourage the addict to remain in treatment. With careful use of the appropriate combinations of new and tried-and-true medicines, in partnership with the rest of a comprehensive treatment program, the odds that addicts can lead happy and productive lives are greater than ever.

Medicines for Withdrawal Stabilization (Detoxification)

Patients and their families are often very excited about the new medicines to assist people in recovery, forgetting that medicines are also important tools for helping addicts through the withdrawal phase—in some cases, they are vital. This review of the withdrawal phase will familiarize you with the symptoms and appropriate medicines so you can discuss them with your physician.

A quick note on nomenclature. Most people use the words "detoxification" or "detox" to refer to the process of separating addicts from their substances of choice. Many treatment professionals prefer to call this process "withdrawal stabilization," so that's the term I'll use in this discussion. The goal of withdrawal stabilization is to safely reduce the uncomfortable withdrawal symptoms and help you through what can be a very difficult period as the brain adjusts to life without continuous infusions of the abused substance.

What Is Withdrawal?

Withdrawal consists of the physiological and psychological processes and changes that the body experiences when the substance of abuse is not available anymore.

Nearly every substance of abuse directly or indirectly acts in the brain's "pleasure center" (the VTA/nucleus accumbens). There, it either stimulates the release of dopamine or enhances its activity, thus triggering intense feelings of pleasure. But there's a price to pay for the wonderful feelings, for substances of abuse also cause changes in the brain that tend to lessen the alcohol or drug's effects over time. As a result, taking the substance again and again causes less and less stimulation of the VTA/nucleus accumbens. The substance gradually loses its pleasurable effects until eventually you experience no euphoria at all—unless you increase the dosage. Where originally it may have taken two beers to produce a feeling of euphoria, after a while four or five are needed, and eventually nine or ten, to produce the same effect. This phenomenon is called tolerance. Think of it as having to feed the "pleasure monster" more and more and more to keep it happy—and prevent it from getting angry.

The physical and emotional signs and symptoms of withdrawal appear when the substance of abuse is suddenly discontinued or decreased in dosage. The symptoms are usually the opposite of those caused by the substance. For example, alcohol consumption depresses the central nervous system, calming you down, putting you to sleep, making you feel at peace, and suppressing brain activity. But alcohol withdrawal stimulates the central nervous system, causing excitement, agitation, sleeplessness, and seizures. Depending on which substance you abuse and how long it stays in the body, withdrawal symptoms can appear within a few hours, days, or even weeks after you stop or cut back.

Withdrawal symptoms vary significantly from person to person, but there are patterns related to the fact that the VTA/nucleus accumbens have grown accustomed to receiving a great deal of the substance of abuse, and thus a great deal of stimulation. With the stimulatory effects gone, a "great silence" descends on the pleasure center. The VTA/nucleus accumbens slow down, causing depression, anxiety, and cravings for the alcohol or drug.

And if the withdrawal symptoms are extreme, they can help drive you to continue using the substance despite significant harm—the definition of addiction.

Medicines for Alcohol Withdrawal Stabilization

Alcohol quiets the brain by interfering with the normal processes that tell cells when to become excited and when to quiet down. Its overall effect is to slow activity within the central nervous system. During withdrawal, the opposite occurs as the sudden lack of alcohol sends the system into overdrive. Moderately severe withdrawal can cause increased production of the adrenal hormones cortisol and corticotrophin releasing factor (CRF), both of which can be toxic to nerve cells. Moreover, cortisol can damage neurons in the hippocampus, a part of the brain thought to be particularly important for memory and control of emotional states. Repeated, untreated alcohol withdrawals may lead to direct damage to the hippocampus, resulting in memory and emotional problems, as well as seizures. Usually, each successive alcohol withdrawal episode is more severe and more complicated than the previous one, as the brain injury becomes more cumulative.

The signs and symptoms of alcohol withdrawal usually appear within the first twenty-four to forty-eight hours after stopping the heavy, prolonged drinking of alcohol. Withdrawal symptoms vary depending on how much, how often, and how long you have been drinking. They may include stomach distress, anxiety, irritability, tremors, sweating, headaches, weakness, difficulty thinking, fever, and seizures. In more severe cases you may suffer from delirium tremens (DTs), a syndrome that includes delirium, profound confusion, hallucinations, paranoia, and life-threatening increases in blood pressure and heart rate.

Patients may experience none, some, or all of the above symptoms at various times after their last drink. The most intense alcohol withdrawal symptoms generally peak at thirty-six to forty-eight hours after the last drink and are usually finished by five to seven days after your last drink.

The DTs

The most severe, highly dangerous syndrome resulting from alcohol withdrawal is known as delirium tremens (DTs). The syndrome includes:

- difficulty sustaining attention
- profound confusion
- clouding of consciousness (disorientation, not knowing who or where you are)

- disorders in the way the world is perceived (hallucinations, paranoia)

- severe, dangerous, life-threatening increases in blood pressure \and pulse rate; the entire cardiovascular system becomes seriously unstable.

Fortunately, DTs usually occur only after a very long period of chronic heavy alcohol use.

Symptoms generally appear within the first forty-eight to ninety-six hours after either completely stopping or significantly reducing (by at least 50 percent) your daily intake. DTs are usually the only lethal effect of alcohol withdrawal—although seizures or a very weak heart can also lead to death—and should always be treated as a medical emergency. If someone begins to get confused or disoriented during the withdrawal process, he should receive immediate medical attention in an emergency room. The syndrome is very treatable if caught early, so only about 10 percent of patients who do get DTs die.

It is critical that a chronic drinker stop drinking only under the direction of an appropriately trained physician who can identify and properly treat DTs. Those who have already experienced DTs with a previous alcohol or benzodiazepine withdrawal, as well as those who have an acute medical illness such as an infection, are more likely to develop DTs, so they should be watched extra carefully.

The majority of patients undergoing alcohol withdrawal can be treated on an outpatient basis. Usually a benzodiazepine—either a long-acting one such as Librium (generic name chlordiazepoxide) or Valium (generic name diazepam), or a short-acting one such as Serax (generic name oxazepam) or Ativan (generic name lorazepam)—is used to stabilize certain brain neurotransmitter receptors.

An antiseizure medication such as Neurontin (generic name gabapentin) or Trileptal (generic name oxcarbazepine) may also be used to make withdrawal more comfortable by reducing anxiety and increasing sleep, as well as safer by decreasing the risk of seizures.

Certain vitamins are needed to help the brain heal, but alcoholics are commonly vitamin-deficient. Therefore, the B vitamins thiamine and folate (folic acid), as well as a multivitamin, may be prescribed to help treat and prevent further progression of the brain and body damage caused by these deficiencies.

The specific dose and frequency of medication and vitamins will be determined by your physician, who will take into account how long you have been using alcohol, the amount you've been consuming every day, your past withdrawal symptoms, current medical conditions and body weight, other drugs you are taking, and your current psychiatric condition.

How long it takes for your withdrawal symptoms to subside will depend on your overall health, as well as the severity and duration of your addiction.

Medicines for Opiate (Narcotic) Withdrawal Stabilization

Depending on which opiates were abused and for how long, the signs and symptoms of opiate withdrawal can include anxiety, restlessness, irritability, sweating, tremor, sneezing, anorexia, nausea, diarrhea, abdominal cramps, sleep disturbances, an altered level of consciousness, and collapse of the cardiovascular system. These problems vary in severity and duration depending on the specific drug dose and duration of use. How long it takes for the withdrawal symptoms to appear also varies; for example, in heroin abusers they typically occur six to ten hours after the last injection, whereas methadone addicts may not experience withdrawal symptoms for over forty-eight hours after the last dose.

In general, the opiate withdrawal stabilization procedures resemble those used for withdrawal from sedatives: longer-acting opiates are substituted for shorter-acting ones and the patient is stabilized on the longer-acting opiate medication, such as Suboxone. The patient will be most uncomfortable during the first one to three days of the opiate withdrawal phase, so a combination of clonidine (an alpha-adrenergic agonist), a benzodiazepine such as Ativan (generic name lorazepam), and a nonsteroidal anti-inflammatory such as Motrin (generic name ibuprofen) is frequently combined with the longer-acting opiate to help make the patient more comfortable for the first two to three days of the conversion to Suboxone. Usually after day three of the correct dose of Suboxone, a patient's withdrawal symptoms and opiate cravings have almost completely subsided.

Medicines for Stimulant Withdrawal Stabilization

Stimulant withdrawal signs and symptoms vary in severity and duration depending on specific drug, dose, and duration of use. They usually begin to occur within twenty-four hours of the last dose of stimulant. Potential symptoms include anxiety, chronic fatigue, irritability, difficulty concentrating, nausea, diarrhea, excessive hunger, depression, lethargy, and significant problems with memory and thinking.

Since no life-threatening physiological reactions occur upon withdrawal from stimulants, a comprehensive supportive treatment program including referral to a local AA/NA group is usually adequate. Inpatient hospitalization and medications are usually not required.

A physician might prescribe Provigil (generic name modafinil) once or twice a day to help with the lethargy associated with the stimulant withdrawal, during just the first one to two weeks of sobriety.

Medicines for Benzodiazepine and Barbiturate Withdrawal Stabilization

Benzodiazepine and barbiturate withdrawal symptoms are similar to those seen with alcohol withdrawal. Potential symptoms include aches and pains, numbness and tingling, irritability, rapid breathing and heart rate, insomnia, tremors, seizures, and changes in brainwave patterns. There is also the risk of suffering the potentially toxic syndrome of delirium tremens. The withdrawal syndrome for long-acting benzodiazepines such as Valium and barbiturates such as phenobarbital may not begin until several days after you stopped using the drug, for it takes a while for these drugs to clear from your body.

With mild benzodiazepine/barbiturate withdrawal, you typically only see restlessness, anxiety, shakiness, and intermittent weakness—but these can often be accompanied by dizziness upon standing, nausea, cramps, and vomiting. These symptoms may be similar to the anxiety symptoms for which the benzodiazepine or barbiturate medication was initially prescribed. Oftentimes, the return of significant anxiety during the withdrawal phase causes sedative addicts to relapse early in the process.

The objective of sedative withdrawal is to stabilize the withdrawal symptoms by giving the patient a long-lasting sedative at a selected dose, then gradually lowering the dose in order to "wean" him or her off the medication. For example, if you were abusing Xanax, you might be given the longer-lasting Klonopin in order to reduce the withdrawal symptoms by making them less severe and more gradual. Which medicine to use and at what dose and for what length of time will be left to your physician's discretion.

Medicines for Hallucinogen Withdrawal Stabilization

Commonly abused hallucinogens such as LSD, mescaline, and PCP have no obvious, consistently evident withdrawal symptoms, so withdrawal stabilization treatment is not necessary.

Although marijuana is considered by many to be nonaddictive, it does have withdrawal symptoms. For a daily user, these occur approximately twenty-one to twenty-two days after marijuana was last smoked. Marijuana withdrawal symptoms include agitation, irritability, insomnia, anxiety, and sweating. Although there are no medicines specifically for marijuana withdrawal stabilization, I often prescribe a low dose of Seroquel (generic name quetiapine), a medicine used for schizophrenia and bipolar disorder that can reduce anxiety and cravings. I have also suggested antidepressants such as Lexapro and Zoloft to reduce anxiety and depression.

What to Do If Your Doctor Doesn't Prescribe the Latest Medicines

This new information about medicines for both addiction and withdrawal stabilization is exciting and valuable, but many physicians, the "recovering" community, and society still tend to resist integrating the new findings into mainstream medicine. They look disparagingly upon the idea of "treating drug addiction with drugs." (Indeed, some physicians adamantly refuse to consider prescribing any medicines for addicts.)

If your healthcare provider, counselor, sponsor, or family members resist the idea of using medicines to treat your addiction, you might try these arguments.

1. New scientific research conducted in the last twenty years makes it increasingly clear that addiction is *not* a weakness or a moral failing. Instead, it is a chronic medical disease with many similarities to other chronic diseases, such as diabetes, hypertension, and asthma. The disease of addiction damages the brain, causing changes that can be documented via MRIs and other imaging tools, changes that firmly, inevitably alter both thoughts, behavoir, and brain function.

2. Alcohol and addictive drugs physically transform and damage the brain, just as excess cholesterol alters and damages the linings of the arteries. This means it's simply not enough to talk to people with addictions and urge them to change their behavior. Most of them can't do that, no matter how much they want to, until their bodies have repaired the physical damage to their brains.

3. An improved understanding of the neurobiological (brain) mechanisms that maintain substance dependence (addiction) has allowed physicians to create more effective combinations of medications and psychosocial treatments in order to improve

treatment outcomes. Thanks to the latest scientific research, there are now anti-addiction medications that provide a key component of genuinely effective treatment by rebalancing the brain's bio-chemistry in ways that make it almost impossible for many people with addictions to experience a high if they relapse and take the addictive substance.

4.   The combination of anti-addiction medication and talking therapy produces significantly better results than talking therapy alone. Now that we understand that addiction is a chronic disease, and now that we have medications to help correct the brain damage it causes, we have a whole new way of thinking about addiction and addiction treatment. With the judicious use of new medicines, many people with addictions can more effectively focus on and benefit from their group and individual therapies, and they can stick to their 12-step programs much more effectively.

5.   This evolution in understanding and treatment is similar to what we saw with other chronic medical illnesses, including diabetes, hyperten-sion, and asthma. Once the scientists studying those life-threatening illnesses invented a breakthrough medication, such as insulin, Lasix, or theophylline, these previously "untreatable" illnesses became conquer-able. Today, we almost can't imagine treating diabetes without insulin or high blood pressure or asthma without at least one, if not two, of a large stable of cutting-edge medications now available. It is almost malpractice these days if a physician treats a patient with one of those illnesses with only behavioral or lifestyle change and management rather than these plus the latest scientifically developed medications.

After presenting these arguments to the "anti-medicine" parties, you might encourage them to buy this book or encourage them to visit www.Enter Health.com/HealingtheAddictedBrain so they can do some investigation on their own. However, if after all of this they are *still* resistant, you will need to look elsewhere for your support to create a successful recovery program.

A Few Final Words

Addiction is a chronic, lifelong disease, and treatment with medication alone cannot serve as a cure. However, when combined with behavioral or other psychosocial therapies, as part of the science-based comprehensive treatment approach to alcohol/drug addiction, pharmacological treatment can be amazingly effective in countering the destructive effects of the drug on the brain and behavior, relieving withdrawal symptoms, and reducing cravings. For most patients, this relief from cravings jumpstarts their recovery program and allows them to concentrate on learning healthy coping skills.

Key Points Review

- Recent scientific advances have made available new medicines that help people resist their cravings while speeding repair to the parts of the brain damaged by addicting substances.

- For maximum success, a comprehensive, science-based treatment program should combine the judicious use of select medicines with a 12-step program, talking therapy, and other tools to help the addict develop healthy thinking and living skills.

- Physicians have new treatments and protocols to help people remain sober.

- The medicine Vivitrol, given as a monthly injection, reduces the urge to use and makes it almost impossible for an alcoholic/opiate addict to enjoy the high that normally comes from drinking or using opiates.

- Vivitrol can reduce the number of "drinking days" per month from fifteen to less than one!

- The medicine Campral helps restore balance among certain brain neurotransmitter systems, especially the GABA system (self-soothing), thus helping to repair the addiction-damaged brain.

- For cocaine and methamphetamine addiction, finding effective medications to reverse the brain damage caused by stimulants has proved difficult despite many scientific research studies. Yet, several different medications show significant promise, including a new vaccine for cocaine addiction.

- Physicians have numerous medicines to help their patients withdraw safely from alcohol and drugs.

- Alcohol and sedative (benzodiazepine and barbiturate) addicts have a 10 percent chance of experiencing DTs during their withdrawal process—therefore, these two types of withdrawal need close supervision of a physician, as 10 percent of the addicts who get DTs die.

- Although new medicines offer new hope to millions of addicts, they are only part of the comprehensive treatment for addiction, a lifelong chronic illness that can be successfully managed but never completely eliminated.

CHAPTER FIVE

Your 12-Step Recovery Program

Recovery is *not* simply refraining from drinking or using. While it does include a lot of "don'ts", recovery is really an action program packed with "do's"—things you *can* do to ensure a happier, more productive and satisfying life through sobriety. One of the best places to learn how to incorporate the "do's" while turning away from the "don'ts" is the 12-step support group. Support groups provide a safe environment in which you can discover new ways of dealing with your illness, share your triumphs and setbacks with others, exchange information and stories, and gain strength from the knowledge that recovery *is* possible.

Twelve-step programs teach methods of dealing with cravings, and they can train addicts to avoid the substances and associated triggers that can cause the cravings. These programs can also provide you with coping skills to help you deal more effectively with problems in all the areas of your life that have been corrupted by addiction, including:

- *psychological* —dealing with depression and other ailments
- *family*—handling marital fighting or separation, dealing with being a noncustodial parent
- *legal*—dealing with divorce or legal issues related to your addiction

- *medical*—facing up to and getting treatment for malnutrition, liver disease, hepatitis, and other diseases associated with addiction

- *social*—developing a network of sober friends and acquaintances, learning to socialize while sober

- *employment*—dealing with repercussions of addiction-driven problems at work, finding new employment

Although 12-step programs do not offer medical treatment or advice, the coping tools you master in these groups can help you remain sober long enough for your body to begin to repair the brain damage caused by the addiction, and for you to adopt the healthful diet and exercise habits that will improve your overall health.

This chapter looks primarily at the 12-step group Alcoholics Anonymous, for this group is the model for so many others, including Narcotics Anonymous, Marijuana Anonymous, Overeaters Anonymous, Cocaine Anonymous, Gamblers Anonymous, and Rational Recovery. Most of the ideas and practices used in AA apply to these groups as well. Depending on your addiction and situation, you may do best in AA, a different group, or both AA and another type of group.

Alcoholics Anonymous—The Model for 12-Step Groups

Alcoholics Anonymous (AA) is a voluntary, worldwide fellowship of men and women from all walks of life who come together to become and remain sober. The only requirement for membership is a desire to stop drinking.

AA was founded in the 1930s by two men who were unable to conquer their own alcoholism through either psychiatry or medicine. They saw, however, that some people had been able to overcome their alcohol addiction with the aid of certain self-help principles. The two men developed AA to introduce these principles to alcoholics. Since then, AA has spread around the world, while its self-help principles and general philosophy have been adapted for use by people suffering from drug addiction, compulsive gambling, overeating, and other problems.

One of the great benefits of AA is that it can truly help an alcoholic come to the realization that he or she is an addict. Most people are unwilling to admit this: no one likes to think that they are physically and mentally different from their peers who are able to drink socially and responsibly. It is not surprising that your drinking career has been characterized by vain attempts to prove that you can drink like other people. The idea that somehow, someday you will control yet still enjoy your drinking is the great obsession of every abnormal drinker. The persistence of this illusion is astonishing. Many pursue it to the gates of insanity or death.

Ultimately, you cannot be successful in your recovery efforts unless you admit to your innermost self that you are an alcoholic. This is the first step in recovery, a step that AA hammers home.

AA's Basic Concepts

AA is a program of total abstinence based on the here and now, on today's struggles, stresses, and cravings. Members work to abstain from one drink, one day at a time. Sobriety is achieved and maintained through sharing experiences, strength, and hope at group meetings, and through working the Twelve Steps for recovery from alcoholism. AA is also a safe, sober environment in which to practice and enhance many of the new coping skills you learn in your treatment program.

Meetings are essentially groups of recovering people helping each other to stay sober and are designed to complement rather than replace the treatment program. The process is anonymous, meaning that what is said in the meetings and between members is kept in confidence; the fact that someone participates in AA is not disclosed or discussed with anyone, at any time, outside the meetings.

AA provides an instant network of supporters who are aggressively focused on becoming sober and remaining abstinent. This is important, for people who are active in their addictions often scare or drive away nonusing friends and family members, leaving them without a support system. AA offers a support system composed of people who have been where you are now, who understand what you are thinking and why your struggle is so difficult. They don't judge or lecture you; they simply seek to support you.

Remember that AA is *only* interested in helping you become and remain sober through the voluntary use of their 12-step program, group support, and individual sponsorship. AA does not follow up or try to control its members, dispense medical or psychiatric advice, prescribe or sell medications, offer religious services, provide drying-out or nursing services or sanitariums, give any welfare or social services, dispense domestic or vocational counseling, or write letters of reference to parole boards, court officials, social agencies, or employers.

AA is not an agency; it is simply a group of people committed to helping themselves and others live sober lives.

Sponsors: Your Guide to AA and Building a Sober Life

The first few weeks and months of recovery are frustrating, confusing, and frightening. There will be many times during this difficult period when people in recovery need to talk about problems and fears. That's where a sponsor comes in.

Your sponsor is your guide to AA, and more. He or she is also the one you call on when that terrible urge to drink hits, you're depressed, sad, just had a fight with your spouse, or have had a slip or lapse. Sponsors do many things, including:

- helping the newcomer by answering questions and explaining the 12-step recovery process

- agreeing to be available to talk and listen to your difficulties and frustrations, and to share their own insights and solutions

- making recommendations and suggestions for handling your problems, based on their personal experiences with long-term sobriety

- confidentially listening to your addiction-related secrets and guilty feelings

- warning you when you step off the path to recovery. Sponsors are often the first to know when you slip or relapse, and will urge you to attend more meetings or get help for problems

- offering guidance as you work through the Twelve Steps

Forty-seven-year-old Sophie came to my institute for help after the latest in a long line of relapses. She had been abusing alcohol for twenty years and had participated in three different alcoholic treatment programs. She had never taken (or been offered) any anti-addiction medications, and her longest period of sobriety was four years. When I asked her what had helped her the most to stay sober in the past, she immediately replied, "AA. Especially my sponsor, Linda. She was always there for me. I can't count the number of times I was just about to have a drink when I'd call her and she'd talk me out of it and give me strength. It really helped to get advice from someone who'd had her own struggles with alcohol and knew what it was like. Without her I wouldn't have been able to go for more than a few days without a drink, but she helped me stay sober for four whole years. Then I stopped going to AA and ended up drinking again."

A sponsor can be invaluable, giving you exactly the motivation you need to stay with the program and maintain your sobriety. You might be assigned a sponsor, or you might choose your sponsor yourself. Look for one who:

- has several years of sobriety from all mood-altering drugs

- has a healthy lifestyle free from struggles with major problems or addiction

- is an active and regular participant in 12-step meetings and who actively works the steps.

- you can relate to. You may not always agree with your sponsor, but you need to be able to respect him or her.

- is *not* a candidate for sexual or romantic entanglement. Heterosexuals should choose a sponsor of the same sex or a homosexual person of the same or opposite sex, while homosexuals should choose either a nongay person of the same sex or someone of the opposite sex.

The procedure for asking for a sponsor varies from group to group, but it's never complex. When you begin going to the meetings, arrive early and ask the leader how sponsors are selected. Some of the techniques are:

- You tell the leader you would like a sponsor, and he or she recommends certain members.

- You put your name on a list at the beginning of the meeting and a prospective sponsor finds you sometime during or immediately after the meeting.

- The leader asks who needs a sponsor; you raise your hand and a potential sponsor comes over to introduce himself or herself.

- The leader asks who is interested in being a sponsor; you see who raises a hand and decide whom you would like to approach.

You don't have to worry about picking the wrong person and being saddled with a sponsor who is not as helpful as you would like. All sponsors are temporary by definition; you have a chance to see if you can work closely together before deciding to make them your regular sponsor. If your temporary sponsor is not right for you, do not hesitate to ask for another. Don't worry about offending your temporary sponsor. Remember, your goal in selecting a sponsor is to get the most you can out of AA.

The Twelve Steps

The heart of AA is its twelve principles for managing sober life. Known as the Twelve Steps, these principles are the group's guidelines for achieving and maintaining sobriety. The Twelve Steps, written in the form of simple statements, are:

1. We admitted we were powerless over alcohol—that our lives had become unmanageable.

2. Came to believe that a Power greater than ourselves could restore us to sanity.

3. Made a decision to turn our will and our lives over to the care of God as we understood Him.

4. Made a searching and fearless moral inventory of ourselves.

5. Admitted to God, to ourselves, and to another human being the exact nature of our wrongs.

6. Were entirely ready to have God remove all these defects of character.

7. Humbly asked Him to remove our shortcomings.

8. Made a list of all persons we had harmed, and became willing to make amends to them all.

9. Made direct amends to such people wherever possible, except when to do so would injure them or others.

10. Continued to take personal inventory, and when we were wrong, promptly admitted it.

11. Sought through prayer and meditation to improve our conscious contact with God as we understood Him, praying only for knowledge of His will for us and the power to carry that out.

12. Having had a spiritual awakening as the result of these steps, we tried to carry this message to alcoholics, and to practice these principles in all our affairs.

Justin, a thirty-one-year-old music producer, told me the low point of his life was waking up in jail after an all-night cocaine binge with no memory of what had happened the night before. Since that particular incident, which had occurred six months earlier, he had been fired from his job, separated from his wife of five years, and lost his house. Justin said he had finally realized that he was powerless to control his cocaine use and that it was ruining his life. So he looked up Narcotics Anonymous in the phone book and went to his first NA meeting. There he learned that he had just taken the first step of NA's 12-step program: admit you are powerless over the addiction and that it is destroying your life. He was on his way toward sobriety.

Participants work through the Twelve Steps with the aid of their sponsors. This can take a long time, so don't be alarmed or frustrated if months or years pass before you accomplish all twelve. Remember that you probably have been using for years, so you can't expect to recover overnight, or even in a couple of weeks.

Although the Twelve Steps ask a lot of God, AA is not a religious organization, nor does it require members to be religious or to believe in God. Instead of being religious, AA is spiritual, and the spiritual choices members make are very personal and individual. Everyone decides what the concepts of God and Higher Power mean to him or her. It is entirely possible to be an atheist yet still participate in and fully benefit from AA.

12-Step Tips

Working through the Twelve Steps requires self-control, soul-searching, and facing up to shortcomings—and this can be difficult for people used to hiding behind alcohol or drugs. AA has developed some short sayings that help people in their day-to-day efforts to stay sober. These include:

- *One day at a time*—This is a key concept in staying sober. Don't obsess about staying sober forever; just focus on today. The goal is do whatever it takes to go to sleep tonight without having used alcohol or drugs today.

- *Turn it over*—Sometimes addicts jeopardize their recovery by tackling problems that cannot be solved. Letting go of these issues—oftentimes by turning them over to a higher power—lets you focus on staying sober and is a very important skill.

- *Keep it simple*—Learning to stay sober can get very complicated and seem overwhelming if you let it. Don't make this process more difficult than it is or has to be.

- *Take what you need, and leave the rest*—This applies to your attendance at AA meetings. It's not a perfect program, and not everyone benefits from every single part of the meetings. However, if you focus on the parts that you find useful, rather than the ones that bother you, you'll get something out of the meetings.

- *Bring your body; the mind will follow*—The most important aspect of 12-step programs is attending the meetings. It takes a while to feel completely comfortable. Try different meetings, try to meet people and read the materials, but just go and keep going.

- *HALT*—This acronym is a shorthand way of reminding recovering people that they are especially vulnerable to relapse when they are too Hungry, Angry, Lonely, or Tired.

Perhaps the most important of these tips is "one day at a time." At the beginning of treatment, it's very common to feel that you are being asked to make countless changes and rework your entire life immediately. You can easily feel overwhelmed by the sheer volume of serious problems that need to be addressed, including: "How am I going to get my job back?" "Will my spouse ever forgive me?" "How am I going to get through the rest of my life without ever taking a drink?" and "How can I rebuild my relationship with my kids?" Trying to tackle all of these problems immediately and simultaneously is far too much, even under the best of circumstances. So keep it simple, especially at the beginning, and just focus on one goal: make it through today (and tonight) without drinking alcohol or using drugs. If you can do this, you are one day closer to a successful recovery.

Going to Meetings is Key!

Many of my patients ask if they have to go to the meetings: can't they simply work through the Twelve Steps on their own?

AA provides you with the support network that is absolutely essential to your recovery. Remember, when you were active in your addiction you felt overwhelmed by stress, work, family, finances, and other aspects of daily life. Intentionally or not, you used alcohol or drugs to insulate or protect yourself from your stress—which meant isolating yourself from your family, friends, coworkers, acquaintances, and others who either contributed to your stress, or who did not approve of, or even attempted to interfere with, your addiction. You did so thinking that this would reduce your stress, not realizing that it would actually generate many more problems and a great deal more stress.

Now that you are sober, you don't have your substance of choice for "protection." At the same time, your brain and body are still healing, so you do not feel your best. You're still prone to falling back into old habits. Your support network is likely still in tatters; many family members and old friends may wish to hold you at arm's length. You need close, instant, and nonjudgmental support, which you can find at AA.

Some people want that support but are afraid to attend meetings, fearing that revealing their inner fears, shames, and secrets to a roomful of strangers would be incredibly intimidating and impossibly stressful. That's a reasonable fear, but you don't have to pour out your life and troubles to a group of strangers right away—or ever. You don't have to say anything at an AA meeting, unless you are moved to do so. Once you attend a few meetings, however, listen to other people talk about their own issues and see the overwhelming amount of support that they receive, you will become more comfortable within the group.

If you are fortunate enough to get into an addiction treatment program, it is critical that you begin going to AA *while* you are in the treatment program, rather than waiting until you complete the program. This way, if you are uncomfortable going to AA meetings or for some reason you do not like a particular meeting, your treatment counselor can help you deal with these issues. Then, when you have finished your treatment program, you will be comfortable with and secure in your AA group, making that group an invaluable resource for you going forward.

Some patients in recovery programs argue that going to treatment and AA at the same time is too much of a burden. (Of course, if they calculated all the time they had spent getting and using their substances of choice, they would realize they had invested a tremendous amount of time in their disease. It's not unreasonable to expect to spend at least that amount of time learning to stay sober.) They say that they don't have time for both, or that they'll begin AA as soon as they finish the treatment program. Even good-intentioned addicts can fall into this trap, which typically leads to one of three things:

- When they finish the program, they *still* feel they are too busy to attend AA meetings.

- When they finish their program, they feel they do not need AA because they are now sober.

- They had fears generated by cognitive inaccuracies that were not addressed in treatment (*i.e.*, "people will laugh at me"). When their treatment is complete, they are still too frightened to face a group of strangers, so they continue to avoid AA meetings.

All of these situations raise the risk of relapse.

That's the primary reason I tell my patients that it is essential to attend AA meetings while in treatment, for that is the best and most reliable way of quickly establishing the support network that is essential to recovery. It's almost impossible to separate going to AA from working through AA's Twelve Steps, for it is extremely difficult to work through the steps on your own. You may enjoy temporary benefits from doing the steps by yourself, but it is very unlikely that you will develop a truly successful recovery program.

There's another reason that going to AA meetings is important, and that is time. Due to financial considerations, most addiction treatment programs only last four to eight weeks. That may sound like a long time when you enter into a program, but it is impossible to completely overcome addiction in one or two months—even six months or a year. Addiction is a lifelong chronic disease that requires lifelong commitment. Unless you're prepared to pay for years or decades of treatment, the only place to go for that kind of continual care is AA. Think of how many years you suffered in active addiction: you'll need to focus intensively on sobriety for at least that amount of time.

Look upon AA as your long-term companion and guide. Just as a dietitian can help you modify your diet and successfully live with your diabetes, hypertension, or obesity/weight loss, AA can help you modify your life, thoughts, and behaviors and maintain sobriety.

Try to be open to what AA has to offer. There are social, emotional, and spiritual benefits. There are practical benefits as well, such as filling up empty slots in your daily schedule (remember that free time can act as a trigger for cravings). AA is a safe place to go during and after your recovery program, a place to meet other people who don't use alcohol or drugs. It offers emotional support and provides you with a worldwide, around-the-clock support network.

Although some people are able to stay sober with only treatment and can forgo AA, the majority of AA members who attend regularly are able to remain sober longer.

Types of AA Meetings

AA meetings are simple and straightforward, they don't require a lot of preparation, and the only participation required of you is to show up, sit down, and open your mind. You needn't speak or reveal anything, or comment on what others say, unless you want to.

There are different types of AA meetings:

- *Speaker meetings*, featuring a recovering person who tells his or her personal story of alcohol or drug use and recovery

- *Topic meetings*, in which a specific topic such as fellowship, honesty, acceptance, or patience is discussed among the group

- *Step/tradition meetings*, where the Twelve Steps and a related set of Twelve Traditions are discussed

- *Big Book meetings*, focusing on reading a chapter from the Big Book (the AA "Bible"), followed by group discussion

Some of these meetings are open to outsiders so the nonalcoholic public can learn about AA, while others are closed to non-AA members.

Finding AA Meetings

There are a variety of ways to find a meeting. You can get contact numbers for local AA groups from directory information; ask for a list of meetings from your doctor, therapist, or counselor; or get a recommendation from someone who is already attending AA. Look on the Internet at www.alcoholics-anonymous.org for online information on meetings and locations. There are also directories that list meetings by city, addresses, and meeting times, as well as offering information about the meeting (is it nonsmoking, men or women only, homosexual or straight, and so on).

Which Recovery Group Is Best for You?

AA is the "granddaddy" of recovery groups, with meetings all over the United States and the world: AA meetings are even held on cruise ships.

There are also many alternative groups offering successful, long-term group support for recovery.

It is perfectly reasonable—in fact, it is a good idea—to try different organizations and meetings before settling on your "home group," or the meeting you will attend regularly. Some AA members have more than one home group, while others prefer to stick with a single group. Others go to AA and another organization, perhaps Narcotics Anonymous, because they are addicted to more than one substance and wish to address both problems simultaneously.

Each group has its own personality, mix of group members, focus, and other factors that make it just right—or not right at all—for you. Finding the best meeting for you is like going to different dealerships to select just the right car. Some people like a Saturn, others a Pontiac or a BMW. But even all the BMW lovers are not of the same mind, for they have different preferences regarding color, audio system, sports package, and so on. You will probably have to go to several different meetings of different groups such as AA or NA or CA, at different locations at different times to determine where you feel most comfortable. On average, a person in recovery will try four to six different 12-step groups before finding just the right fit. (Some people striving to recover from alcohol addiction find they are more comfortable in a particular NA meeting, and vice versa. That's fine.)

A Few Final Words

Sometimes you'll feel like everything is hopeless, and sometimes you'll be too tired to participate. Sometimes your family will need you, and sometimes you'll have an important appointment. There are many reasons why you won't want to go to 12-step meetings or work the program—many distractions and endless excuses.

Always remember that going to your meetings and continually working the program is helping to keep you sober, safe, and sane. Go to your meetings. Keep working the program. If you have nothing to contribute and feel you're too tired to get anything out of your meeting, go anyway. Just show up! Keep showing up. Remember, your goal is to learn to live clean and sober by doing, not just by "not doing."

Key Points Review

- AA and similar programs are designed to introduce addicts to the principles of self-help so they can develop a lifestyle focused on recovery and sobriety.

- AA meetings do not replace treatment; rather, they are groups of recovering people helping each other to stay sober.

- Now that you are sober, your substance of choice (alcohol or drugs) can no longer "protect" you from the stresses of life.

- You can find a new kind of protection in the understanding and support offered by fellow addicts at AA.

- AA provides an instant network of supporters who are abstinent and committed to maintaining that abstinence.

- AA offers the Twelve Steps, guiding principles that help a recovering addict remain sober and healthy.

- Sponsors help newcomers by answering questions and explaining the 12-step recovery process, being available to talk and listen to your difficulties and frustrations, sharing their own insights and solutions, making recommendations and suggestions, discussing addiction-related secrets and guilt feelings, and helping keep others sober.

- Besides the original Alcoholics Anonymous meetings, many addicts also find other kinds of 12-step groups helpful, depending on their substance of choice, including Narcotics Anonymous (NA) and Cocaine Anonymous (CA).

- Many alternative 12-step groups that are not based on the concept of a Higher Power include similar options for sobriety and rational recovery. They include self-help approaches that focus on personal responsibility, personal empowerment, and strength through a sober social network.

CHAPTER SIX

Dealing with Difficult Emotions

Emotions are the feelings you experience throughout the day, every day—feelings such as happiness, sadness, relief, anger, joy, and fear. It is often difficult for addicts to identify their emotions early in the recovery process, which makes it harder for them to feel comfortable, relate to others, and remain sober. Unhappy emotions such as depression, anxiety, and anger are particularly problematic for addicts: emotional distress or disconnect is one of the primary reasons they begin to drink or use again.

Back in the "good old days," you had an easy way to deal with painful, bewildering, and scary emotions like depression, anxiety, and anger: have a drink or get high. It was quick, simple, and temporarily effective. You may not have known how to handle these feelings any other way; you may have confused them with cravings. Mostly, you just wanted them to go away. Using drugs or alcohol was a quick way to change bad feelings into good ones, ease anxiety, blot out depression, and hide the pain. However, now that you're sober, you must face up to and deal with these unpleasant feelings when they surface during recovery and in daily living.

This can be difficult, for most addicts are out of practice dealing with emotions; they often have trouble even naming the emotions they experienced during their years of addiction. Now that they're in recovery, they are often unaware of the fact that they are experiencing normal, everyday emotions: instead, they think that what they're feeling is a craving. Added to that is the fact that alcohol and drugs can change the way the brain works and scramble emotions. So during recovery, you may feel irritated or wonderful for no reason other than the unresolved brain damage.

Emotions occur whether you want them to or not: they are a normal part of being human, and they are neither "good" nor "bad." By applying what you learn in this chapter and elsewhere in this book, especially Chapter Two, *you can learn to control your feelings and emotions, as well as your reactions to them.* Suppose, for example, an irresponsible driver cuts you off, forcing you to slam on your brakes to (barely) avoid an accident. Many people would be angry; that's perfectly natural. But while some would scream, curse, chase the other car down, and cut him off to "teach him a lesson," others would choose to tune the radio to a soothing music station and let the negative emotion fade away. Unfortunately, people with addictions tend to have difficulty dealing with strong emotions without the "help" of their substances of abuse. Indeed, they often interpret the emotion as a signal to begin drinking or using, forgetting that they have choices: do or do not become angry, do or do not drink or use. That's why it is vital that you learn to recognize emotions as they arise and to handle them safely. This is not easy, but it's certainly possible and absolutely necessary if you want to maintain your sobriety.

In this chapter, you'll learn how to identify and deal with three of the most troublesome, uncomfortable emotions: depression, anxiety, and anger. You'll learn how to distinguish negative feelings brought about by the recovery process from those normally experienced as part of everyday life. And you'll learn to recognize and work through your negative feelings using the thought-based tools and concepts discussed in Chapter Two.

Depression

Tom, a fifty-seven-year-old computer programmer, had struggled with depression for years. He was naturally pessimistic about life and seemed to have no energy or motivation. Sometimes he'd become very irritable for no apparent reason. Other times he'd find himself crying without understanding why. Although Tom felt tired practically all the time, he had a great deal of trouble sleeping. During his twenties, Tom discovered that amphetamines could chase away his blue feelings and make him feel great, at least temporarily. Unfortunately, once he came down from the high, Tom felt even worse than before. And as he continued using amphetamines to treat his depression, he noticed that the periods of relief seemed to get shorter while the number of pills he needed grew larger. It wasn't long before Tom found himself saddled with a drug habit.

It is not unusual to feel sad, blue, or depressed from time to time. Sadness is a normal reaction to loss, life's struggles, or injured self-esteem. Sometimes, however, these feelings are so intense and long lasting—usually lingering more than a month—that they interfere with your ability to think, work, eat, sleep, enjoy being with others, or care for yourself. This is referred to as major depression, a true psychological/neurological disorder caused by a chemical imbalance in certain neurotransmitter systems in the brain. Depression is common among addicts during the recovery process, often related to the actual depressant effects of alcohol or drugs or to the family, job, financial, and other problems caused by drinking or using. It saps your energy, reduces your motivation to change, and increases your feeling of hopelessness, all at the same time. Unfortunately, many seek solace in alcohol and drugs once again, and lapse or relapse. However, returning to drinking or using is not an effective means of coping with depression, for it only serves to make you more depressed in the long run. By definition, depressive disorders include feelings of helplessness and hopelessness, and the negative thinking that is associated with depression can make it very difficult for someone to take the steps necessary for recovery.

Other symptoms of depression include:

- feeling low in energy

- overeating or not eating

- having sad thoughts

- stopping normal activities, such as work, cleaning house

- losing interest in your career or your hobbies

- sleeping more than usual or having difficulty sleeping

- losing interest in sex

- having increased thoughts of drinking or using

- stopping your exercise program

- avoiding social activities

- feeling bored, irritable, or angry

- having crying spells

- having suicidal thoughts or actions

Are You Depressed?

Many people don't realize they are depressed, for there is no single, easily identifiable feeling of depression and because the neurochemical changes occur so slowly, many of the symptoms sneak up on you. Indeed, if you are depressed you may think the problem lies "out there" rather than within you. Oftentimes, it's only when you consider how you feel about yourself, others, and the world, as well as how you feel physically, that you realize you are depressed. In other cases, you only realize you are depressed when other people notice it and tell you.

Are You Depressed?

Listed below are eighteen symptoms of depression. During the last month, how often did the following statements apply to you?

1	2	3	4	5
Never	Rarely	Sometimes	Often	Always

_____ 1. I feel hopeless.

_____ 2. I am overwhelmed by feelings of sadness or grief.

_____ 3. I feel worthless.

_____ 4. I take no pleasure in the things I used to enjoy.

_____ 5. I sleep way too much or way too little.

_____ 6. I am not excited about things the way I used to be.

_____ 7. I am in a bad mood.

_____ 8. I feel agitated or antsy.

_____ 9. I am a skeptical or pessimistic person.

_____ 10. I don't have any energy.

_____ 11. If I want something done right, I feel I have to do it myself.

_____ 12. I feel angry for no apparent reason.

_____ 13. I don't expect others to treat me with respect.

_____ 14. I feel guilty for no apparent reason.

_____ 15. My appetite has changed recently.

_____ 16. Things seem like just too much effort.

_____ 17. I take my anger out on others.

_____ 18. I have no energy.

If you marked that you "often" or "always" experienced more than five of the symptoms listed above during the last month, but the symptoms did not last for the entire month, you are probably suffering from depression. But if you experienced more than five and the symptoms lasted the entire month or longer, you are probably in the midst of a major depressive episode. If you think that you may have major depressive disorder (MDD), talk to your physician as soon as possible to find out for sure.

Causes of Depression

Several factors can cause depression or make it more likely that you will experience depression. They include:

- history of depression in the family
- grieving the loss of a loved one
- personal disputes, such as conflict with a family member
- physical, sexual, or emotional abuse, now or in the past
- major life changes such as moving, graduating, changing jobs, getting divorced, getting married, or having a baby
- serious illness, your own or that of someone close to you
- substance addiction

Experiencing just one of these can trigger depression, but your risk of depression goes up exponentially as more of these factors come into play.

Sometimes stress is the cause. We live in a time of rapidly increasing social, technological, demographic, and economic change, and the demands made upon us to adjust are taxing. The stress of having to adapt to so much in a brief period of time can wear you down; you can lose your resiliency and find it difficult to bounce back from adversity. You begin to pull away from others, your energy decreases, and you fall into depression.

There are other causes of depression, including a wide variety of medicines and medical issues such as heart disease, cancer, and diabetes. Indeed, depression is one of the most common complications of chronic illnesses such as diabetes and cancer. Be sure to have your physician give you a thorough physical examination in order to see if your depression is caused by disease or medications.

Managing Depression

Depression is a problem in its own right and a particularly severe problem for the recovering addict, since depression and other negative mood states are a major reason for relapse. Of course, returning to drinking or using is not an effective means of coping with depression, for it only serves to make you more depressed in the long run.

Depression, whether it be "normal" depression that clears up on its own or major depressive disorder that requires medical evaluation and treatment, is a risk factor for addiction and for a return to the addiction. It's important that you get treatment, if necessary, and that you master ways of dealing with depression without using alcohol or drugs.

Following are several coping skills that have proven to be helpful in managing mild to moderate depression. (These can also be helpful as part of the treatment for major depressive disorder.)

1. Increase your awareness.

When you are active in your addiction, you are unaware of important information in the world around you, as well as inside your own head. Be on the lookout for signs of an impending depression so you can take steps to ward it off.

- Pay attention to your mood changes. When you start to feel sad, gloomy, ashamed, bored, lonely, or rejected, tune into what's going on. These are important clues to your thinking.

- Own your feelings. If you are having trouble recognizing your feelings, start talking about them. Tell someone just how you are feeling at any given moment.

- Be alert to your body language. This is a clue to your emotions. Notice your posture, your facial expression, how you are walking and moving.

- Label your avoidance. Keep a lookout for (sober) people, places, and activities that you once enjoyed but are now avoiding. Don't try to analyze the reasons; just be aware that you are avoiding them.

- Watch for times when your confidence disappears. Are there times and places when you feel inadequate or lean on others for help? Ask yourself whether you were able to handle this particular task on your own before. Remember, a loss of confidence can be a symptom of depression.

- Look for activities that take great effort. Do you have to force yourself to make or return phone calls? Do you have trouble completing tasks around the house? One of the symptoms of major depression is lethargy and decreased interest in activities. You simply do not feel like doing things anymore, even those things you used to enjoy.

- Become aware of times when you have trouble concentrating or making decisions. Do you vacillate over simple decisions or second-guess yourself? Both can be signs of depression.

Remember, everyone experiences some of these symptoms at one time or another; that's completely normal. Problems arise when either individual symptoms are pushing you toward relapse or you're suffering from more than one at once.

2. Change your way of thinking about yourself and the world.

A prime characteristic of depression is the tendency to view the world and yourself through inaccurate and depressive perceptions. As we discussed in Chapter Two, the way you think affects the way you feel, so it's important that you examine your thoughts to discover ways they may be contributing to your feelings of sadness and depression. To do this you must first become aware of your self-defeating thoughts. Then ask yourself why you are having these thoughts. Finally, replace these inaccurate, depressing thoughts with healthier, more realistic ones, and act on the new thoughts. If you follow these steps, you can go a long way toward overcoming the symptoms of depression.

3. Use problem-solving techniques.

One way to deal with depression resulting from inaccurate, negative thoughts is to use a general problem-solving technique. This can help you feel that you have an impact on and control over your problems. As you put the problems into a different perspective and begin solving them, depression begins to fade, and you will start to feel better about yourself.

 A great way to learn good problem-solving skills is to take the Problem Solving e-lesson in the Advanced Recovery section on www.EnterHealth.com/HealingtheAddictedBrain.

4. Change your activity level.

When you are depressed, you do less, blame yourself for doing less, and become even more depressed and apathetic. Increasing your activity level is a major way to change both your thinking and your feelings. Activity improves mood, counteracts fatigue, increases motivation, and sharpens mental ability. And most likely, others will respond positively to your attempts to become more active, providing reinforcement for continued change. Whenever possible, exercise, go to a movie or ball game with a friend, participate in social or religious activities, and otherwise engage in life. Studies show that even very depressed people feel better when they become more active.

5. Make a plan.

How do you become—and remain—involved in activities? Make a plan.

- Become task-oriented. In general, you can schedule three kinds of activities: things you must do daily (eating, dressing, getting the kids ready for school, etc.); things that give you pleasure (going to a movie, reading a good book, etc.); and things that bring a sense of satisfaction (answering phone calls or letters, finishing a project). Remember that your primary goal is to follow the schedule you establish for yourself. The focus is on becoming more active.

- Stick with the plan, but stay flexible. Make sure your plan allows for alternatives if the activities you planned suddenly fall through. For example, if you planned a trip to the zoo but it rains, instead of getting down in the dumps, go to a movie. Then get on with the rest of your schedule.

- Schedule activities in half-hour to one-hour increments. A six-hour trip to the local museum is way too much for one activity. If you make it too long or too complex, it will be tempting to skip the activity altogether. On the other hand, fifteen minutes of filing your nails may not provide enough activity. Thirty to sixty minutes is a good length of time for an activity.

- Don't get too specific or too general. Instead of shopping for a certain color of nail polish, simply plan on going to the mall for one hour. Just getting out and walking through the mall is more important than going to a specific store looking for a particular item. (However, doing the latter is better than doing nothing at all.)

- Plan for quantity, not quality. When you are depressed, remember: anything worth doing is worth doing poorly. If you go bowling, getting a 75 is as good as rolling a perfect 300, if it gets you out of the house and out of your depressed mind-set. If you golf, scoring 150 is as good as making par. The important thing is that you're doing something.

- Pat yourself on the back. After completing a planned day of activities, analyze what you have done. Look at what you did right, and see where you can improve. If you completed the majority of tasks you planned, congratulate yourself and set new goals for tomorrow.

If you have difficulty developing the motivation to draw up a plan, ask a (sober) friend for help. He or she can select activities and perhaps even accompany you on one or two to get you started.

Here's the activity plan one of my patients made. It looks simple, but it was effective!

My Activity Plan

Date: Tuesday, August 12

Activity #1: Go to mall, buy ice cream cone, window shop while eating it

Alternative: If mall is too busy, get ice cream bar at store and walk around the park

I'll remind myself: All I have to do is eat ice cream, which I love, and window shop, which I love doing

I'll know I'm successful if: I enjoy the ice cream and the walk

Activity #2: Read Princess Diana book for 30 minutes

Alternative: Read "Enquirer" for 30 minutes

I'll remind myself:	I've always enjoyed reading, I like this
	particular book, I'm reading strictly for
	enjoyment, not to memorize it and pass a test
I'll know I'm successful if:	I get into my reading and the time
	passes quickly

Plan two activities for yourself every day, using copies of the "My Activity Plan" form or a form of your own design. Do this every day for several weeks, and you may find that your depression eases significantly!

 You'll find printable copies of the "My Activity Plan" worksheet on www.EnterHealth.com/HealingtheAddictedBrain.

6. Interact with others.

Being with people can be very useful, for it helps to draw you out of your isolation and get you engaged in conversation and activities. Try to be with other people. Confide in someone, tell them how you're feeling (but don't burden them with overly lengthy recitations of your problems). Let your family and friends help you. They don't have to try to cheer you up, simply be with you.

7. Be optimistic yet realistic.

It's easy to conclude that you'll never be happy again, but with time and the right treatment there's a good chance you'll cheer up. Look forward to being happy again, but expect your mood to improve gradually over time. Feeling better takes time, and people rarely snap out of a depression. You'll feel better day by day, but in the meantime postpone important decisions until your depression has lifted. Before deciding to make any significant change or transition—such as taking a new job or getting married or divorced—discuss the situation with others who know you well and have a more objective view of your situation.

> *Tom, the computer programmer I talked about at the beginning of this chapter, was eventually able to put a stop to his amphetamine use by using modafinil to reduce his withdrawal, enrolling in an outpatient treatment program, and regularly attending AA meetings. But he also needed to get a handle on his depression. To this end, Tom wisely decided to focus on changing just one thing: his activity level. He joined a gym, set up a workout program with the help of a trainer, and made a commitment to exercise every single day for at least twenty minutes, if not longer. After following his workout program for just a couple of weeks, Tom noticed a definite increase in his feelings of well-being, improvement in his concentration, and a decrease in stress. As an added bonus, he was sleeping better than he had in years—which in itself made the change worthwhile. While Tom still had a long way to go before gaining control of his depression, he had put one piece of the puzzle into place.*

If You Still Feel Blue...

Sometimes a depression is too severe to be handled by these tools, and sometimes it is related to a physiological ailment. If your depression persists even after you have worked your way through these tools and techniques, ask your physician if you're a candidate for therapy or antidepressant medication.

Anxiety

Anxiety is fear, agitation, or unease that arises when you feel that something threatening is looming. The threat might be specific, like an upcoming speech you have to give, or it could be general, perhaps the ups and downs of everyday life. Whatever the cause, anxiety triggers physical, mental, and emotional reactions such as worry, nervousness, and unwarranted fear.

Everyone feels anxious at times, but people with addictions may feel it even more intensely, especially during recovery. So much is riding on the success of the recovery: jobs, family, income, self-esteem. Your anxiety level can skyrocket as you ask yourself "Can I do this?" "Will I ever recover completely?" And life's everyday stressors not only start the anxiety cycle, they can help to keep it going perpetually.

Anxiety can greatly increase the risk of relapse for two reasons. First, anxious feelings are unpleasant, and it's natural to want to do something to make them go away. For those who are accustomed to using drugs or alcohol to blunt or mask their anxious feelings, the urge to drink or use can become overwhelming. Secondly, addicts often misinterpret anxiety as cravings and feel that they absolutely must use in order to make the craving (anxiety) go away. Unfortunately, many people in recovery are unaware that they are anxious or that they may even have a full-blown anxiety disorder.

Causes of Anxiety

Although the exact cause of anxiety isn't known, several factors can contribute to it. They include:

- history of anxiety in the family

- irregular levels of neurotransmitters in the brain

- certain personality types

- stressful life situations

- certain negative experiences during childhood

- medical conditions (such as an overactive thyroid gland)

- coping with a serious illness

- chronic conditions such as diabetes or high blood pressure

- excessive caffeine use

Any of these can bring about temporary or long-lasting anxiety. First and foremost, see your physician to rule out any medical conditions. Once a physician has ruled out or treated underlying medical conditions, try the techniques for breaking the anxiety cycle I describe beginning on page 135.

Are You Suffering from Anxiety?

Listed below are eighteen symptoms of anxiety. During the last month, how often did the following apply to you?

1	2	3	4	5
Never	Rarely	Sometimes	Often	Always

_____ 1. My muscles feel tense or sore.

_____ 2. I feel somehow detached from myself.

_____ 3. I feel shaky or dizzy.

_____ 4. I'm afraid of going to shopping malls and other public places.

_____ 5. I have trouble concentrating.

_____ 6. I am uncomfortable speaking or performing in front of others.

_____ 7. I flush or blush a lot.

_____ 8. I worry about losing control of myself or my life.

_____ 9. I avoid going to social events.

_____ 10. I have feelings of impending doom or fear of dying.

_____ 11. I perspire a lot.

_____ 12. I have feelings of dread.

_____ 13. I bite my fingernails or pick at my cuticles.

_____ 14. I'm afraid that I will embarrass myself or lose control in front of others.

_____ 15. I have trouble falling or staying asleep.

_____ 16. I feel immobilized and unable to act.

_____ 17. My breathing is shallow and rapid.

_____ 18. I anticipate the worst-case scenario.

Any symptoms that you marked "sometimes," "often," or "always" should be warning signs that you are experiencing anxiety. Once you recognize that you're becoming anxious, try to pinpoint what might be causing your anxiety. Writing in a journal every day can be a helpful way to zero in on when your anxiety starts to flare and what may be triggering it.

The Self-Perpetuating Cycle of Anxiety

Anxiety occurs as part of a cycle that, unfortunately, can become vicious and self-perpetuating. It begins with stressors. A stressor is anything that elevates adrenaline and triggers the stress response. Loud noises, heavy traffic, arguments, money problems, illness, and divorce are just a few examples of stressors.

Perhaps the stressor of the moment is a financial one: you don't have enough money to handle your bills, and you're worried about it. As the stress becomes more intense, you fall into negative thinking patterns, telling yourself, "Oh, man, I'm a failure. I don't make enough money, because I didn't study hard enough in school and now I have a lousy job." These thoughts ratchet up emotional and physical symptoms of anxiety: your stomach begins to grind, your head aches, and your neck muscles tighten up. Now you're not only worried, you feel uncomfortable and unwell, two additional stressors.

This conglomeration of stressors makes you even more nervous, irritable, and unsettled, which leads to more negative thinking and more emotional and physical symptoms of anxiety. The anxiety cycle has not only been perpetuated, it's been intensified.

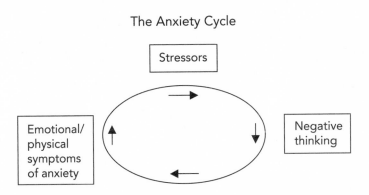

The Anxiety Cycle

Ana is a good example of someone caught in an anxiety cycle. When the monthly bills came, she and her husband Jake would often argue about Ana's spending habits. He thought she threw money around, while she thought that she purchased only what was necessary. The real problem, she said, was that everything was too expensive these days. The argument would escalate, and Ana would be flooded with feelings of anger, tension, and depression. Her heart would pound, her hands would shake, and she'd feel like she was burning up. "I can't handle these feelings," Ana would tell herself. "I've got to have a drink." Then one drink would lead to three or four, and Jake would get furious with Ana for drinking too much. He'd slam the door on his way out and wouldn't return for hours. Ana, in the meantime, would require even more drinks to quell her steadily rising anxiety levels.

Breaking the Anxiety Cycle

Even if you realize that your anxiety and fears are excessive and irrational, decreasing them is not a simple matter. Depending on the type and severity of your anxiety, you may require assistance from a qualified therapist to overcome your reactions to the situation you fear. This "talking therapy" may also be combined with nonaddicting medications to reduce the severity of your negative reactions. A therapist may also recommend social skills training, participation in a support group, and relaxation and stress management training.

Whether working with a therapist or on your own, you can take steps to break the anxiety cycle by doing the following:

1.   Increase your awareness of what's causing your anxiety.

2.   Challenge and change the negative thinking that keeps the anxiety cycle in play.

3.   Manage stress.

Let's take a look at each in more detail.

1. Increase your awareness.
Before you can take steps to decrease your anxiety, you must figure out what's causing it. Certain situations, people, places, times of day, and thoughts can set the stage for forms of anxiety that range from a little bit of nervousness to a full-blown panic attack. Use the following techniques to discover what's pushing your buttons. Once you find out, you'll be in a much better position to change things for the better.

- *Keep a journal*—Keeping a journal is an excellent tool for discovering when and why your anxiety tends to arise. Once you understand what sets your anxiety off, you'll be in a much better position to defuse it or even prevent future bouts.

- *Write in your journal several times a day*—Each morning, afternoon, and evening, write down the time of day, the place, what you're doing, and your current thoughts and feelings. You may also want to rate the intensity of your feelings from 0 to 10, with 10 being the most intense. Make additional entries in the journal whenever you feel anxious. Over time, the journal should reveal certain patterns that contribute to your anxiety.

- *Assess the control factor*—When analyzing an anxiety-producing situation, ask yourself if it is something that you have control over. You have some control, for example, over the anxiety you may be feeling about your bills: you could budget your money more effectively, eat out less often, get rid of your cell phone, or buy fewer clothes. But in some situations you have no control. You may, for example, become anxious when a person you're attracted to doesn't return your interest. Then you just have to realize that you have no control over the other person and that you must let it go. Trying to change the inevitable will simply increase your anxiety and get you nowhere.

2. Challenge and change negative thinking.

Your thoughts affect your feelings. Your feelings, in turn, influence your actions. This is especially true regarding anxiety. Your thoughts can cause your anxiety levels to skyrocket, inflaming the urge to drink or use. Or they can calm you down considerably and help you stay on the sobriety track. Therefore, recognizing your pro-addiction thoughts and changing them to pro-recovery thoughts is an essential step in easing anxiety.

If anxiety is making you feel worried or fearful, you may be thinking, "If I have a drink or a hit, I won't feel so crummy anymore. Yeah, okay, the relief will only be temporary, but any relief is better than none." Use the techniques you learned in Chapter Two to replace that pro-addiction thought with health-enhancing ones such as these:

- "Using alcohol or drugs to relieve my anxiety is dangerous."
- "I can handle this feeling and I can discover what is causing it."
- "I don't have to tolerate this feeling; I can get control of the thoughts that are causing it."
- "Once I've managed my feelings of anxiety, I will feel stronger."
- "I can and will learn how to control my thoughts, feelings, behaviors, and beliefs so I won't have to go through this prolonged anxiety anymore."

Changing the thoughts that arise in response to anxiety will help you control your anxiety.

3. Manage stress.

There are many strategies and techniques for releasing and reducing stress and thereby lowering anxiety levels. Some of the most helpful include:

- *Exercise*—Aerobic exercise (the kind that gets your heart pumping and increases your respiration) is an extremely effective anxiety-buster, relieving muscle tension, burning up stress hormones, and stimulating the release of endorphins, the body's feel-good hormones.

- *Relaxation techniques*—Given the way nervous system is designed, it is physically impossible to be stressed and relaxed at the same time. That's why practicing relaxation on a regular basis is the best way to lower your anxiety level and give your body and mind a "vacation" from stress. There are many good relaxation techniques, including yoga, meditation, progressive muscle relaxation, deep breathing and visualization. There are also some effective hands-on relaxation therapies such as massage, acupressure, and reflexology. Find the ones that work best for you.

- *Simplify your life*—Many people are stressed out because they have too many responsibilities and roles to fill but too little time. Try these tips:

  o Figure out the most efficient and least stressful ways to do what has to be done.

  o Make a "to do" list with the most important things at the top, the less important things beneath.

  o Plan ahead to decide how to combine activities; look for shortcuts.

  o Cross off any activities that you can skip.

  o Do one thing at a time to increase efficiency and decrease the stress of multitasking.

o Develop realistic goals.

o Delegate tasks: you really don't have to do it all yourself!

o Learn to say no. It's all right to let people know what you can and can't handle—for whatever reason.

- *Take care of your body*—An undernourished, exhausted, or under-exercised body is a stressed body. Eat a healthful, balanced diet, get plenty of rest and sleep, and exercise for at least an hour every day.

- *Utilize your support system*—Friends, family, individual therapy, group therapy, or community support groups can help you get through the rough patches and validate your successes. Use them.

- *Enjoy yourself*—Don't neglect having fun! Take time to do the things you enjoy with people you enjoy. Do things that feel good to you. Distract yourself when you're stressed by having fun.

For those with the "regular" anxiety often seen in recovery, the three steps described above—increasing awareness, changing negative thinking, and managing stress—will be enough to keep the problem under control. More severe cases will require medications and psychological counseling in addition to these three techniques.

Breaking the Anxiety Cycle

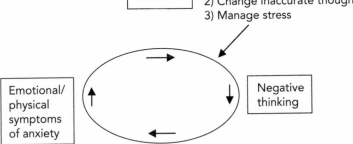

Planning the Break

Whether you're under the care of a physician, a therapist, or on your own, it helps to think through then write down the ways you'll break your anxiety cycle. Here's what Ana, the woman who drank in response to money arguments with her husband, decided to do:

Breaking My Anxiety Cycle

1. Increase awareness—Keep a journal, making notes on what's happening, what I am thinking and who I am with when I feel anxious or crave a drink. Fill out a "Test of Thought Accuracy" form to see if my thoughts are innacurate.

2. Change inaccurate thoughts—Change inaccurate thoughts to accurate thoughts instead of drinking away my anxiety. Remind myself that I'm upset, but I'm not going to drown my feelings in alcohol. I'll do some deep breathing exercises instead, then sit down and talk with Jake about the best way to deal with this problem.

3. Find new ways to manage stress—Do breathing exercises every day, take restorative yoga class three times a week. Walk and ride a bicycle daily. In an emergency, take a hot bath and think things over before doing anything rash.

4. Find healthy solutions to the problem at hand—Working with Jake, make a budget and agree on fair amounts to spend on household. Also, talk to financial advisor. Get treatment for alcoholism.

In the list below, write down ideas for breaking the anxiety cycle that you plan to try within the next week. You can use any of the suggestions above or make up your own.

Breaking My Anxiety Cycle Worksheet

1. _____
   _____
   _____

2. _____
   _____
   _____

3. _____
   _____
   _____

4. _____
   _____
   _____

5. _____
   _____
   _____

 You'll find a printable copy of the "Breaking My Anxiety Cycle" form on www.EnterHealth.com/HealingtheAddictedBrain.

Carry your "Breaking My Anxiety Cycle" form with you. When you begin to feel anxious, read your list and pick one strategy that you can use immediately.

Any healthy recovery program requires a lot of change on your part. Change is difficult, and the mere process of change can trigger anxiety. If your anxiety does return, look upon it as an opportunity to review your anxiety management plan and renew your commitment to taking care of yourself.

Be prepared to deal with the possibility that anxiety symptoms will return. If they do, they will probably not be as intense or long-lasting as they were before because you are learning new skills to manage your anxiety. Also, remember that everyone has anxiety at times; it is a normal part of life.

Anger

Anger, that unpleasant feeling of annoyance, resentment, or rage you experience when a goal is blocked, your needs are frustrated, or you are attacked, is one of the most basic human emotions. It's with you from birth to death and can be an asset or a liability, depending upon how it's used. On the positive side, anger can help you survive assaults, correct injustices, grow, become independent, and establish better conditions. But it can also destroy property, relationships, and lives, if it's not handled properly. And banishing it is supposedly a major reason that many people drink or use drugs: you have probably used your substance of choice as a way to get your anger under control or to calm yourself down after an angry outburst or argument. Unfortunately, it only works in the short term, if at all. The expression of anger can take many forms, including:

• yelling

• physical violence

• sarcasm

• verbal attacks

- crying

- teasing

- depression

- rejection

- pouting

- vengefulness

- silence

- suicide

Causes and Effects of Anger

There are five general sources of anger:

- fear for your own or someone else's safety (either real or imagined)

- loss or threat to your power and control

- an insult to your pride (the implication that you or someone close to you is substandard)

- an insult to your self-sufficiency and autonomy (the suggestion that you don't have the ability to do things on your own)

- an insult to your self-esteem or status

Anger spurs the release of adrenaline and other chemicals in the bloodstream. These chemicals, in turn, cause the following physical reactions:

- faster heart rate

- increased blood pressure

- tense muscles

- dry mouth

- headache

- upset stomach

- increased perspiration

Uncontrolled Anger Sequence—Looking at the Thoughts Within
We experience anger in our own unique ways, but there are some common patterns seen with uncontrolled anger. It begins with a trigger: something unpleasant happens. Let's say you were about to pull into a parking space when someone else cut in front of you and got to it first. Certain thoughts arise as you evaluate that person's behavior and think about what happened. "Jerk!" you cry. "Unfair! Terrible! Awful! He shouldn't do that!" You respond emotionally to your thoughts with feelings of being outraged, offended, and, ultimately, hopeless about changing the situation. This prompts you to act out your feelings with certain behaviors—you pound your steering wheel, roll down your window and yell at the offending driver, and (if you're really out of control) hit the gas and ram his car.

You can map the uncontrolled anger sequence like this:

Situation (Being cut off) → Thoughts (Jerk! Terrible!) →
Emotion (Outrage) → Behavior (Road rage)

In most cases, there are consequences to pay: you may feel guilty, the other guy might get out of his car and come after you, or you may be sued. And these consequences can escalate your anger and perpetuate the cycle. The upshot of the uncontrolled anger sequence is that you actually feel worse and find yourself in an even more difficult situation.

Managing Anger

As you learned in Chapter Two and saw in the example above, uncontrolled anger is the result of inaccurate thoughts. And these thoughts may arise so naturally or so often that you don't even recognize them. To manage anger effectively, it's essential that you learn to think differently about the things that normally make you angry. Once you change your thoughts, your emotions and behavior will follow suit. Please note that the goal is not to entirely eliminate anger, for sometimes it can be helpful. The point is to learn to identify anger, decide whether it is justified, and then either control it or use it to your advantage. This is a challenge for those in recovery, for the addiction causes brain damage and inaccurate thinking that triggers unnecessary anger.

The five major techniques that will help you manage your anger are:

1.   Change your thinking about the situation.

2.   Look at the situation from the other person's perspective.

3.   Ask yourself if your thoughts are accurate.

4.   Think of happy or pleasant times in the past.

5.   Think first, speak carefully.

1. Change your thinking about the situation.

When you are angry, your thinking can become exaggerated and overly dramatic. To see how this works, consider the following example:

- *Situation*: Your spouse says he is going to go to a ball game with the folks from his office this evening and will be home around midnight.
- *Thoughts*: You realize you are not invited, and you interpret this to mean your spouse prefers to spend his Friday evening with the same people he spends most of his waking hours with, rather than you.
- *Emotions*: You're hurt because you feel rejected. This quickly turns to anger or even rage.
- *Behavior*: You drink to quell your anger.

Try replacing these inflammatory thoughts with more rational ones. For instance, instead of catastrophizing and saying, "Oh, this is the worst thing, and everything's ruined," remain calm and say to yourself, "This is frustrating, but it's not the end of the world. And getting angry is not going to fix it."

Let's look at the same situation to see how changing your thoughts can change everything else.

- *Situation*: Your spouse says he is going to go to a ball game with the folks from his office this evening and will be home around midnight.

- *Thoughts*: You realize that because your spouse isn't coming home until later, you won't have to prepare dinner. You decide to get some takeout that he normally doesn't like and make plans to use this unexpected extra time doing something enjoyable.

- *Emotions*: You feel happy that you'll be able to start the weekend by doing something relaxing.

- *Behavior*: You decide to take a leisurely bath and pamper yourself and then watch a movie that you've been wanting to see.

In the first example you can see how quickly thoughts can spur anger and possibly trigger a drinking binge. In the second example, controlling your thoughts allowed you to set up a positive scenario that resulted in pleasant emotions and no relapse. While restructuring your thoughts is not easy, it is doable with practice and well worth the time and effort it takes to learn this technique.

Logic (clear thinking) is an excellent tool for defeating anger, because anger, even when it's justified, can quickly become irrational. So use cold, hard logic. Remind yourself that the world is not out to get you; you're just experiencing some rough spots. Try changing your thoughts and applying logic each time you feel anger getting the best of you: you'll get a more balanced perspective.

You'll find more specifics and practice in mastering this valuable anger management tool on www.EnterHealth.com/HealingtheAddictedBrain.

2. Look at the situation from the other person's perspective.

Suppose your friend Amanda said she was going to meet you at a mutual friend's party but didn't show up. Before you get too steamed up about it, try to imagine why she didn't come. Did she have trouble finding a babysitter? Is she under a lot of stress? Could she be sick? You might also ask yourself why Amanda's presence so important to you. Do you have unrealistic expectations for the friendship? Are you making demands that she cannot fulfill? When you look at it from the other person's point of view, you realize that there are perfectly understandable reasons why things may not be exactly the way you want them to be.

3. Ask yourself if your thoughts are accurate.

Accurate thoughts can be supported by facts; inaccurate thoughts cannot. It's important that you start examining your thought processes when anger arises, to test their validity. In order to do this effectively, it is critical that you write your thoughts down, so that you can more easily identify and change any distortions in your thinking. Following are a few examples of inaccurate thoughts:

- "If she really cared, she wouldn't have…"
- "She should have understood what I was going through."
- "He must not want me to succeed if he does this."
- "My parents never let me do anything."

All of these statements would be difficult to prove. Ask yourself if you can back up your thoughts with facts. If you can't, postpone your angry reaction until the facts are clear. Here are some examples of how thought analysis can steer you to accurate thinking:

Thought Analysis

Situation	Inaccurate thought	Accurate thought
Parents kept me from going to a party where there was probably going to be beer served.	My parents never let me do anything.	My parents love me very much. They are just being overprotective. I can deal with that.
I came home from high school and found Mom drunk again, even though she promised never to drink again.	If she really cared, she would not have started drinking alcohol again. I hate her!	Mom has a medical disease. I see that she is really trying. She didn't relapse because she doesn't care about me. Really, her relapse has nothing to do with me.
My wife is always on my back, nagging me to go to NA meetings, calling my sponsor every two seconds. She's always searching through my things to see if I've got a stash.	She doesn't understand how hard this recovery stuff is; she never gives me a break. She's driving me up the wall!	She stayed with me through thick and thin, even after everyone else dumped me. She's understandably worried that I'll relapse. Maybe she's overreacting, but it comes from her love for me.

4. Think of happy or pleasant times in the past.

When you find yourself in an anger-provoking situation, it's helpful to visualize some pleasant scenarios that can help diffuse the anger. Try thinking of the following when you feel yourself losing your fight against anger:

- The first time you fell in love

- The best present you ever received

- Time you've spent with a beloved pet, friend, or family member

- A dream that really came true

- Getting your driver's license and driving solo for the first time

Visualization (imagery) does not appeal to everyone, but if it works well for you, set aside fifteen minutes per day, every day for a week, to practice visualizing pleasant scenarios. (Remember to practice your imagery techniques when you are *not* angry.) Some people find it helpful to list the four or five enjoyable scenarios they have practiced on an index card. When they're angry, they pull the card from their wallet or purse, select one scenario, and start imagining.

Remember why this technique is helpful: if you can concentrate on a pleasant scene, you may be able to stop the negative thought patterns that trigger uncontrolled anger. Once you have calmed down, you can analyze your inaccurate thoughts and create accurate thoughts to replace them.

5. Think first, speak carefully.

Angry people tend to jump to conclusions, some of which can be very inaccurate. If you find yourself in a heated discussion, slow down and think through your responses. Don't say the first thing that comes into your head. Listen carefully to what the other person is saying, and take your time before answering.

Listen, too, to what is underlying your anger. Suppose, for example, you like freedom and personal space, while your significant other wants more connection and closeness. If he or she starts complaining about your solo activities, don't retaliate by painting your partner as a jailer or an albatross around your neck. Try to understand your partner's point of view, and help your partner understand yours.

It's natural to get defensive when you are criticized, but don't rush to fight back. Instead, listen to what's underlying the words: the message that this person might feel neglected and unloved. It may take a lot of patient questioning on your part, and it may require some breathing space, but don't let your anger—or a partner's—cause a discussion to spin out of control.

Restructuring Your Thoughts

Read the example below, then restructure the thinking to change the outcome from a negative one to a positive one.

Old Way of Thinking

- Situation: I have a fight with my spouse about my spending habits.

- Thoughts: I'm furious with her for trying to control me. After all, I work hard; why shouldn't I spend my money as I see fit? She's just a gold digger who wants to keep all of my money for herself!

- Emotions: I'm frustrated because someone is trying to tell me what to do. I'm hurt because I feel that I'm only worthwhile because of my paycheck.

- Behavior: I start drinking to ease the anger and the pain.

Now rewrite the scenario to control your anger by managing your thinking. Remember to look at the situation from the other person's point of view, ask yourself if your thoughts are rational, and substitute thoughts of happy or pleasant times in the past.

New Way of Thinking

- Situation: You have a fight with your spouse about your spending habits.

- Thoughts: _____

  _____

  _____

- Emotions: _____

  _____

  _____

- Behavior:_____

  _____

  _____

If, in the end, you did not fly off the handle and you did not turn to drugs or alcohol to escape, you've completed the exercise successfully! Next, think about the last time you got angry, and map out the scenario, as shown above. Then change your thinking to promote a more positive outcome. In the future, whenever you find yourself getting angry, take a moment and jot down what happened and how you could have changed the thoughts to change the outcome. Eventually you'll be able to do this in your head automatically.

Taking Responsibility

When you do something you don't feel good about, your first impulse may be to try to convince yourself and others that it wasn't your fault. For example, you don't really feel good about being violent or abusive, and you know that it was wrong, but you try to deny responsibility for your behavior. Below are some common ways that people deny responsibility for their angry behaviors.

- *Blaming the victim*—"She provoked me." "He made me do it." "She just wouldn't shut up." "If he wasn't such a jerk…" "You know how women are."

- *Justifying the violence or abuse*—"I had the right." "I had no other choice." "I had to." "It was absolutely necessary." "She hit me first."

- *Blaming an outside factor*—"I had a little too much to drink." "I had a really bad day." "There's never any money." "The kids…" "Her parents…" "If it wasn't for…"

- *Minimizing the facts*—"It was only a slap, not real violence." "In all the years we've been married, I only lost it those few times." "It's not that big a deal."

Denying responsibility is an attempt to shift the blame; somehow you become the victim, not the aggressor. But when you see yourself as a victim—of your partner, the system, society, or current circumstances—you give away your personal power. In truth, you are in control of yourself. You choose your emotions, actions, and reactions to both circumstances and the behavior of others. You choose to:

- react to others or to life's experiences in a negative way
- stay in a difficult or destructive relationship
- allow yourself to become angry
- allow yourself to become abusive or violent

However, just as easily you can choose to:

- react to others or to life's experiences in a positive way
- leave a difficult or destructive relationship

- refrain from becoming angry

- refrain from becoming abusive or violent

Although you aren't responsible for everything that happens to you, you are responsible for your reactions. And when you take responsibility for your actions, you put yourself in a position of power, increasing your ability to take charge of yourself and your life.

Seven Steps to Taking Responsibility

One of the best ways to stop anger before it starts is to take responsibility for yourself and your behavior. You can accomplish this by following seven steps:

1. *Make a commitment to change*—The first step on the journey is to define the changes you want to make and decide that you're going to stick with the program and achieve these goals.

2. *Seek relationships and activities that are positive*—When you feel good about your life, you will automatically be less negative and angry.

3. *Take care of yourself*—Self-care lies at the heart of taking responsibility for yourself. Pay attention to your physical, mental, emotional, and spiritual needs.

4. *Broaden your resources and support system*—Surround yourself with supportive people who want you to stay sober. Take advantage of the many organized forms of support that are available: individual therapy, group therapy, 12-step programs, www.EnterHealth.com/HealingtheAddictedBrain, and so on.

5. *Give yourself permission to say no*—Draw clear boundaries, and set limits to protect yourself and your physical, emotional, and financial health. Don't do things just to please others. Otherwise you are likely to feel used, abused, resentful, and angry.

6. *Set realistic, reachable goals*—Think about what you've easily achieved in the past, then set your next goal one step beyond. When you reach this goal, set another slightly beyond it. Don't aim for perfection if you haven't made all the stops along the way. Be sure to pat yourself on the back as you reach each goal.

7. *Let go*—Make peace with yourself concerning situations you can't control, and let them go. This is doubly important if you choose to remain in frustrating situations. Remember that you can only control yourself.

Feel Better Now!

Hopefully, you now understand that your thoughts create emotional reactions that perpetuate stress, depression, anxiety, and anger. In the past, you used alcohol or drugs to deal with these uncomfortable emotional states. But now, by simply changing your inaccurate thoughts into accurate ones, you have the tools to change the uncomfortable and unnecessary emotions of depression, anxiety, and anger and negate the need for mind-altering substances.

You're trying to break long-standing habits, so be gentle with yourself as you are learning these new skills. If you mess up and revert to the nasty behavior you dislike, don't beat yourself up. That only makes things worse. Analyze what went wrong. Tell yourself that you slipped and will be more careful next time. Keep chipping away at the anger cycle; you *will* get better over time.

Make it your task to transform negative moods into positive ones by planning mood-regulating behaviors into your daily schedule. There are lots of mood-regulating behaviors that can help keep you on an even keel, physically, mentally, and emotionally. Incorporate several of the following into your daily life, especially when you have the urge to drink or use. Many of these are also excellent ways to increase your energy level and release tension, nervousness, and anxiety, which is the best approach to turning a bad mood into a good one.

Mood-Regulating Behaviors

- Exercise

- Listen to music

- Talk with a supportive friend

- Watch TV or your favorite video

- Write

- Read

- Go to the park

- Shop

- Soak in the tub

- Practice relaxation or stress-management techniques

- Look at photographs from happy times

- Blow bubbles

- Work

- Take a road trip

- Sing

- Do something silly (skipping, finger painting, playing on a swing)

- Eat

- Talk on the phone

- Go for a walk

- Play with a pet

- Breathe deeply

- Play video games

- Watch or play sports

You can undoubtedly think of other activities you especially enjoy that can help you reduce stress, depression, anger, and anxiety. Add them to the list, and keep this list where you can see it daily. Before you ever take another drink or use drugs, do at least two things on this list. Chances are, you'll find that the urge to drink or use simply melts away.

Key Points Review

- Depression is natural at times, but it becomes a problem when it interferes with one's ability to think, work, eat, sleep, enjoy being with others, or engage in self-care.

- Depression is a major reason for relapse.

- It can be managed by learning to increase your awareness, changing your way of thinking about yourself and the world, using problem-solving techniques, altering your activity level, planning activities into your daily schedule, interacting with others, and being optimistic.

- If you are feeling sad, you will probably suffer from inaccurate thinking. Thus, it is important to learn to create accurate thoughts from the facts of the situation.

- When you feel depressed, you may not want to do anything, but activity will make you feel better.

- Anxiety is a normal reaction to life's difficulties, but for recovering addicts it is dangerous because it can be confused with cravings and trigger a relapse.

- We often make anxiety worse by "feeding" it with negative thoughts.

- You can break the anxiety cycle by increasing your awareness, challenging and changing the negative self-talk that fuels the anxiety cycle, and managing your stress.

- Exercise, relaxation techniques, simplifying your life, taking care of yourself physically, calling on your support system, and enjoying yourself will all help you manage stress and control your anxiety.

- Anger is a normal, healthy emotion. When expressed appropriately, anger helps you let go of stress and frustration.

- You may not be responsible for everything that happens to you, but you are responsible for your reactions and your behavior.

- If you see yourself as a victim of your partner, the system, society, or some set of circumstances, you are giving away your personal power. You are letting "them" make you angry and drive your self-defeating behavior.

- You are in control of yourself. You *always* choose your actions and reactions to circumstances or other people's behavior.

- You can learn to manage your anger by changing the way you think about unpleasant situations, looking at these situations from another point of view, asking yourself if your thoughts are rational, and thinking of happy times rather than focusing on the present unpleasantness.

- Recovery requires a series of hard choices over a long period of time. Fortunately, you can choose to shift your attention away from negative thoughts and toward neutral or even positive ones.

CHAPTER SEVEN

Dealing with Dual Diagnoses

Dealing with addiction by itself is difficult enough, but over half of those with addictions also suffer from emotional or psychiatric disorders such as depression, anxiety disorder, bipolar disorder, or other ailments. If you are one of the millions of people who has such a "dual diagnosis," you must tackle two problems at once. The bad news is that both of these illnesses are brain diseases that can harm you physically, psychologically, socially, and spiritually, weakening your ability to function effectively and relate to others. The good news is that countless people have faced down both of these diseases and come out winners.

Dual diagnosis complicates treatment and increases the risk of relapse, as the two illnesses can interact, each making the other worse. At times, the symptoms of one may overlap and even mask symptoms of the other, making diagnosis and treatment much more difficult. The presence of one illness may also slow your recovery from the other, weakening your resolve to remain sober. That's why it's important to get the correct diagnosis and simultaneous treatment for both.

When One Problem Becomes Two

Simon was a thirty-three-year-old opiate addict who was also strug-gling with bipolar disorder. He had been abusing OxyContin and using heroin for more than nine years. When he was a sophomore in college, he began to show symptoms of depression. Later, he began having delusions (he thought he was God) and would go for days without sleeping, problems that resulted in three hospitalizations over the past ten years. During that same ten-year period he was also admitted to two different detoxification programs for narcotic addiction. Unfortunately, Simon never found a program that would treat both disorders. The psychiatric treatment for his bipolar disorder didn't address his opiate addiction except to refer him to NA after discharge. And the drug treatment program did not include a physician who could help him with his psychiatric problems.

A wide variety of psychiatric illnesses can accompany addiction, including:

- major depressive disorder

- bipolar disorder/mania

- anxiety disorders

- obsessive/compulsive disorder

- attention deficit disorder/ADHD

- sexual dysfunction

- eating disorders

- panic disorder

- phobias

- schizophrenia

There are some general patterns seen in many dual diagnoses. For example, depressive disorders are often linked to both alcohol and sedative use, while bipolar disorder is often seen with stimulant and opiate use. However, nothing is set in stone. Substance abuse or addiction can be found in conjunction with any psychiatric illness, and vice versa.

Sometimes the problem begins with substance use, abuse, or addiction, which grows severe enough to trigger depression, rage, hallucinations, suicide attempts, and other symptoms of a psychiatric disorder. Fifty-three percent of drug abusers and 37 percent of alcohol abusers have at least one serious mental illness. In other instances, it starts with a psychiatric illness. The individual tries to self-medicate, using alcohol or drugs to (temporarily) relieve anxiety, depression, or other psychiatric symptoms. Or perhaps he or she starts by using alcohol or drugs recreationally, but because of the preexisting psychiatric illness, slides more easily into addiction than others might. Either way, 29 percent of those diagnosed with mental illness abuse either alcohol or drugs.

Socioeconomic factors can also encourage addiction in those with mental illnesses, who are often victims of "downward drift." Unable to hold a steady job and maintain strong family ties, such a person can wind up living in a marginal neighborhood where alcohol and drug use is more prevalent. It's easy to get caught up in substance abuse under these conditions. If he or she has trouble developing social relationships, then groups or friendships that are based on alcohol or drug use may become even more attractive.

More Than Two Diseases at Once

Dual diagnosis is not simply a case of one disease added to another: it's one *multiplied* by the other. This makes dealing with either disease a much more complicated matter. The complications can stem from several factors:

- Many symptoms of severe substance addiction mimic those of psychiatric conditions. This means the patient may have to go through withdrawal from alcohol or drugs *before* an underlying psychiatric problem can be accurately diagnosed.

- Withdrawal from alcohol or drugs can trigger symptoms that are much like those of a psychiatric illness, increasing the risk of misdiagnosis.

- Even if the dual problems are correctly identified, it is very difficult to get those suffering from addiction *plus* emotional distress to engage in and cooperate with treatment.

- The erratic, distressing, or dangerous behavior of the dual-diagnosed patient may make him or her unwelcome at home or in community residence or rehabilitation programs. As a result, the person often loses his or her support system and may suffer frequent relapses and hospitalizations.

- Those with dual diagnoses are more likely to perpetrate and suffer from violence, domestic violence, and suicide attempts.

- Untreated chemical dependency can contribute to a recurrence of even well-controlled psychiatric illness.

- Untreated psychiatric illness can contribute to alcohol or drug relapse.

Making matters worse, mental health service programs are not well prepared to deal with patients having dual diagnoses. Typically, a mental health service has separate departments for substance dependence and for mental illness but no department designed to handle both problems simultaneously. As a result, patients often bounce back and forth between departments, or they may be refused treatment altogether because neither department is equipped to deal with them.

Leslie is a twenty-four-year-old alcoholic who also suffers from schizophrenia. On three different occasions she was turned away from treatment when she was in crisis, specifically because of her "other" illness, whether it was alcoholism or schizophrenia. Once, she drank too much and almost died of alcohol poisoning, yet was refused treatment by an addiction program because of her schizophrenia symptoms and the fact that she had been off of her medications for the prior two months. Another time, she was experiencing hallucinations, delusions of grandeur, and confusing thoughts and had not slept in a week. The psychiatric stabilization unit would not admit her because she was an alcoholic, saying she needed to go to a drug treatment program to get sober before they could help her. On all of these occasions, she continued her downward spiral after being denied treatment.

It's important to understand the "other" illnesses before discussing how they're treated, so let's take a look at the major classes of psychiatric diseases that often accompany addiction.

A Look at the Other Half of a Dual Diagnosis

The psychiatric ailments that can coexist with and complicate addiction fall into three general classes:

- mood (affective) disorders

- anxiety disorders

- psychotic disorders

Let's take a brief look at each of the three general classes.

Mood (Affective) Disorders

Moods are part of an affective spectrum ("affective" means relating to, arising from, or influencing feelings or emotions) that ranges from extreme depression on one end to uncontrollable, dangerous elation on the other. All of the mental illnesses within this spectrum are referred to as affective disorders.

Tracking the Mood from Zero to Ten

The Affective Spectrum looks like this:

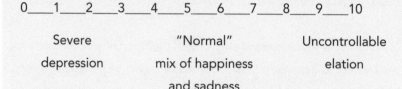

0___1___2___3___4___5___6___7___8___9___10

    Severe   "Normal"   Uncontrollable

  depression   mix of happiness   elation

              and sadness

The mood of a mentally healthy person usually lies in the center of the spectrum, ranging somewhere between 3 and 7 and reflecting the normal ups and downs of life. Sometimes the mood may drop dramatically—when a loved one dies, for example—but it does not stay at 0 or 1. Instead, it moves back to the middle range after an appropriate period of time. The mood may also shoot up occasionally when something wonderful happens, such as the birth of a child, but it soon settles back in the middle range.

With mood disorders, one's mood does not hover around the center of the spectrum. Due to chemical imbalances in the brain, it pushes to the extreme ends of the spectrum for no apparent reason and can stay there for alarmingly long periods of time. The four types of mood disorders are:

- major depression

- mania

- bipolar disorder

- bipolar "mixed" state

Let's take a look at each of these four types in more detail.

Major Depression

Marie was a forty-nine-year-old mother of three teenage children who worked at home part-time as a bookkeeper. Since the death of her fourth child fifteen years earlier, she had suffered from recurring major depression. Even though she was taking two kinds of antidepressants, she still had very disturbing episodes of depression at least once or twice a year. When Marie fell on her front steps during an ice storm and hurt her hip, her family doctor prescribed Vicodin (hydrocodone) for the pain. Marie noticed that not only did the Vicodin ease her pain, it also eased her depression somewhat. When her family doctor would not prescribe any more Vicodin, she went to other doctors to get the narcotic and, eventually, started ordering it over the Internet. Over time, Marie found that it took more and more Vicodin to keep her from going into withdrawal (between thirty and fifty tablets per day), and she noticed that her depressive episodes had worsened. Eventually her depression became so severe that she could not get out of bed and was having suicidal thoughts. She was admitted to an inpatient psychiatric unit for a week to stabilize her depression before beginning outpatient dual diagnosis treatment at my institute.

Everyone feels sad occasionally: feeling hopeless, helpless, and blue from time to time is a normal reaction to life's losses and struggles. The cause of this kind of depression is usually clear, and the low feelings generally resolve themselves over time.

Sometimes, however, the unhappy feelings are extremely intense and long-lasting. They may not be motivated by life events, and they don't dissipate in a reasonable amount of time. Instead, they can linger for months and even years, interfering with one's ability to think, work, eat, sleep, enjoy being with others, and otherwise participate in life. The depressed feelings seem to come out of nowhere or be an extreme overreaction to a problem or situation. Even if the person's life situation improves, he or she continues to feel miserable, helpless, and hopeless, unable to imagine ever being happy again.

These intense, long-lasting symptoms are indicative of an imbalance in brain chemistry; specifically, levels of neurotransmitters such as serotonin and norepinephrine have fallen too low. Instead of "normal" depression, those with this condition have the brain disease called major depression and may suffer symptoms such as:

- sad thoughts

- crying spells

- low energy/excessive fatigue

- cessation of normal activities, such as work or cleaning the house

- loss of interest in career or hobbies

- sleeping more than usual

- insomnia

- increased thoughts of drinking

- lack of interest in physical activities or exercise

- avoidance of social activities

- feelings of boredom, irritability, or anger

- decrease in sex drive

- overeating or not eating

- suicidal thoughts or actions

(At least five of the above symptoms must be present during the same two-month period, at minimum, to qualify for the diagnosis of major depressive disorder.)

Negative moods, sadness, and other symptoms of major depression are common among addicts during the recovery process. The problem may be directly caused by the depressant effects of alcohol or drugs or may be triggered by the loss of a job, family disturbances, and other problems that stem from addiction. Or the symptoms may be due to a chemical imbalance in the brain, the alcohol or drugs themselves, the results of the alcohol or drug use, or all three.

Unfortunately, when in the throes of a major depression, the addicted person may find it especially difficult to participate in a recovery program. When you can't drag yourself out of bed in the morning and feel there's no hope, how are you going to find the energy to attend yet another group meeting?

Mania

Mania, simply put, is the opposite of major depression: an extreme, long-lasting feeling of elation that's way out of proportion to the positive events that seem to have triggered it. Mania is characterized by:

- abnormal excitability
- exaggerated feelings of well-being
- very rapid thinking
- excessive activity, without getting tired
- persistent enthusiasm
- impulsive behavior (*e.g.*, spending sprees, hyperactive sexual drive)
- impaired judgment

The diagnosis of mania is applied to those with a persistently elevated mood or extreme irritability, plus at least three of the following symptoms, for at least one week:

- overly inflated self-esteem
- decreased need for sleep (sleeping less than four hours per night yet not feeling tired during the day)
- increased talkativeness, usually difficult to interrupt
- flight of ideas, often jumping from one unrelated subject to another in rapid succession

- easy distractibility, with difficulty staying on task or following through with projects

- increased goal-oriented activity, such as excessive shopping or sexual activity, or physical agitation (difficulty sitting still)

- excessive involvement in pleasurable and risky behaviors or activities, such as having unprotected sex or shoplifting

A key point about mania is that it's not just feeling *very* happy and energetic. It's extreme, uncontrolled happiness and energy that makes it difficult to engage in normal life activities and encourages reckless, often dangerous behavior that can destroy one's relationships, finances, and health. Patients experiencing a manic episode can also exhibit delusions of grandeur, excessive religiosity, or incorrect beliefs about the world or themselves.

Bipolar Disorder

Also known as manic-depressive illness, bipolar disorder is a serious brain disease that causes extreme shifts in mood, energy, and functioning. In a sense, it is major depression and mania taking turns pushing the mood from one end of the spectrum to the other. Cycles of depression and mania typically recur and may become more frequent over time, disrupting work, school, family, and social life. There is a tendency to romanticize bipolar disorder, for many artists, musicians, and writers have suffered from extreme mood swings. But there's nothing romantic or appealing about a disease that has ruined many lives and, without effective treatment, can increase the risk of suicide.

Unfortunately, people suffering from bipolar disorder tend to stop treatment once the disease becomes stabilized. Feeling normal, they convince themselves that they aren't "sick" and therefore don't have to continue with psychotherapy and medications. Since the symptoms typically don't recur right away, they can easily feel justified in forgoing treatment. Unfortunately, symptoms generally do return quietly and gradually, leading to recurring family, financial, and interpersonal crises.

A bipolar patient may be tempted to use drugs or alcohol to deal with the emotional symptoms. At first, this may seem to be an effective strategy, for bipolar symptoms can be reduced and even hidden during alcohol or drug intoxication. Unfortunately, these substances can destroy neurotransmitter systems and further upset the imbalance in brain chemistry, making bipolar illness even worse over the long run. Increasing amounts of alcohol and drugs will be required to mask these worsening symptoms, leading to an accelerated progression of the disease and possibly hospitalization.

Bipolar "Mixed" State

Odd as it sounds, it is possible to suffer from symptoms of major depression *and* mania at the same time. Symptoms of both must last for at least a week (occurring nearly every day) in order for them to constitute a "mixed" episode. They also must be sufficiently severe to interfere with work or regular daily activities and may include:

- agitation or irritability
- insomnia
- significant change in appetite
- depressive mood at times; elated mood at times
- suicidal or delusional thinking

Complicating matters even further, severe depression, mania, or bipolar disorder may be accompanied by a loss of contact with reality (psychosis). Symptoms of psychosis include:

- hallucinations—hearing, seeing, or otherwise sensing the presence of stimuli that do not exist
- delusions—irrational beliefs, not explained by a person's religious beliefs or culture, that defy normal reasoning and remain firm even in the face of overwhelming contradictory evidence

Anxiety Disorders

Feeling anxious, worried, or fearful from time to time is normal and sometimes even helpful, as it forces a person to consider things carefully and possibly avoid dangerous situations.

But sometimes anxiety becomes excessive and triggers an overwhelming, irrational, possibly paralyzing fear of everyday situations, such as meeting new people, going to a job interview, or even leaving the house. When "normal" anxiety begins to interfere with a person's ability to attend to the responsibilities of everyday life, it has crossed the line and become an anxiety disorder. The disorder can take several forms, including social phobias, panic disorder, obsessive-compulsive disorder, and post-traumatic stress disorder. And while the symptoms of anxiety disorders vary, the central features include:

- episodes of nervousness that are quite severe at times
- fear
- emotional distress
- physical symptoms triggered by intense distress and tension, such as increased heart rate and rapid breathing
- sleep and appetite disturbances—an increase or decrease in either, or a combination of increases at certain times and decreases at other times
- feeling out of control—especially in specific situations such as being in high places or crowded public spaces
- difficulty coping with both stressful *and* normal life situations

In extreme cases, one can experience:

- self-defeating cognitive and behavioral rituals—performing repetitive tasks, such as repeated hand washing or constantly checking the door locks, which temporarily reduce anxiety but serve no other purpose

Anxiety is a serious complicating factor in addiction treatment. Most addicts interpret anxiety as a craving for their substance of choice. Thus, an ongoing, untreated anxiety disorder puts an addict at a very high risk of relapse. Conversely, successful treatment of a coexisting anxiety disorder can significantly increase a person's chances of maintaining sobriety.

Psychotic Disorders

Psychotic disorders are mental disorders (schizophrenia and schizoaffective disorders) that result in a seriously disorganized thinking pattern and impaired contact with reality. The symptoms of psychotic disorders, which are caused by neurochemical imbalances in the brain, include delusions, hallucinations, incoherent or disorganized speech, and disorganized or bizarre behavior. Symptoms of psychotic disorders can also surface in extreme versions of major depression or bipolar disorder.

Delusions are defined as inaccurate or false beliefs a person clings to even in the face of contradictory evidence and logic. Examples include the feeling that someone or something is out to get you (such as the FBI or aliens) or believing that you are someone else (perhaps Jesus or the president of the United States).

Hallucinations, which are defined as internal sensory perceptions (sights or sounds) that don't reflect reality, can be visual, auditory, olfactory (smell), or tactile (touch). Visual hallucinations involve seeing things that are not actually present, such as another person or aliens. Auditory hallucinations involve hearing something that does not exist at that moment, such as the sound of another's voice.

The treatment of dual diagnosis patients with psychotic disorders can be very challenging. In general, the same principles of treating both diseases apply, but treatment is conducted in a coordinated fashion and includes heavy family involvement.

Treating Both Halves: The Dual Diagnosis Program

There are numerous patterns of alcohol or drug dependence that can combine with several types of psychiatric illnesses to produce a wide variety of dual disorders. Treating one half of a dual disorder may relieve the symptoms of the other, to some extent. *But "single" treatment is never enough,* even if the half being addressed is the more severe of the two ailments! In order for treatment to be successful, both halves of the dual diagnosis must be tackled simultaneously with a program that addresses substance abuse or addiction, emotional or psychiatric disorders, and lifestyle issues. This combined treatment plan must be comprehensive, coordinated, integrated, and flexible, and should include:

- treatment for the psychiatric illness
- treatment for the alcohol or drug addiction
- participation in a 12-step program
- appropriate nonaddicting medication for each illness
- family education and participation in treatment for both component illnesses

I can't emphasize strongly enough the importance of seeking a treatment program designed for the dual diagnosis (when it is present), rather than for addiction alone. Treatment programs for substance dependence only are generally *not* recommended for people who also have a mental illness. These programs tend to be confrontational and coercive, but most people with mental illness are too fragile to take such intense emotional jolting. These programs also tend to discourage the use of medication, which is oftentimes crucial to those with psychiatric illnesses. In addition, substance dependence programs may demand abstinence as a precondition for entering treatment. Abstinence is, of course, the eventual goal for all addicts, but many people with dual diagnoses may be in severe denial. They should not have to wait until they own up to their addiction before beginning treatment.

Addressing the Emotional or Psychiatric Disorder

Dual diagnoses can take many forms, so the treatment plan must be as flexible as it is comprehensive and integrated. In addition to offering medications, behavioral treatments, a 12-step program, family counseling, and other standard elements of addiction treatment, the dual diagnosis plan must address the issues unique to each type of psychiatric disorder. The general areas that should be addressed with each type of disorder are as follows:

For major depression (or the major depression component of bipolar disorder):

1. Assess danger to individual and others.

2. Find an environment that is safe from alcohol and drugs and the addict.

3. Assess the need for medications, and determine the appropriate one(s).

4. Improve the addict's problem-solving methodology.

5. Improve coping skills to deal with stress.

6. Encourage and help develop a healthy, sober support system.

7. Resolve issues of loss.

8. Improve self-esteem and feelings of control (restructure the thinking process through cognitive behavioral therapy).

9. Improve eating habits.

10. Manage depression (offer specific treatment for major depression).

11. Provide an addiction treatment program that takes the dual diagnosis into account.

12. Provide education regarding the importance of sticking with the medication.

For mania:

1. Find an environment that is safe from alcohol and drugs for the addict.

2. Use medicines to stabilize the disease, and provide education regarding medication side effects and the importance of staying with the medicine.

3. Teach how to keep the thought processes logical and appropriate.

4. Eliminate delusional or psychotic disturbances.

5. Improve social interaction and decrease isolation via a healthy, sober peer group.

6. Improve self-esteem and feelings of control (restructure the thinking process through cognitive behavioral therapy).

7. Improve sleep patterns.

8. Provide an addiction treatment program that takes the dual diagnosis into account.

9. Offer a psychotherapy program to help integrate all of the above.

For anxiety disorder:

1. Assess the need for nonaddicting antianxiety medication.

2. Identify the source of anxiety and fears.

3. Improve coping skills, especially in stressful situations.

4. Improve problem-solving skills.

5. Improve self-care (exercise, nutrition, health).

6. Improve social interaction and decrease isolation via a healthy, sober peer group.

7. Improve self-esteem and feelings of control (restructure the thinking process through cognitive behavioral therapy).

8. Improve communication skills.

9. Teach stress management techniques.

10. Educate family about anxiety.

11. Educate the addicted person and family regarding medication's side effects.

12. Provide an addiction treatment program that takes the dual diagnosis into account.

For psychotic disorder:

1. Discover and clarify the origin of disorder.

2. Screen for co-occurring psychiatric disorders that may also need to be treated (*i.e.*, major depression or anxiety).

3. Provide appropriate referrals to knowledgeable treatment providers.

4. Consider the use of nonaddicting medication.

5. Educate the addicted person and family regarding emotional and psychological problems and their treatment.

6. Improve coping skills, especially in stressful situations.

7. Improve problem-solving skills.

8. Teach stress management techniques.

9. Improve social interaction and decrease isolation via a healthy, sober peer group.

10. Provide an addiction treatment program that takes the dual diagnosis into account.

11. Educate and involve family in the treatment program.

Remember that these are only general guidelines. Each treatment plan must be tailored to the individual's specific situation and needs. Be aware, however, that any treatment plan that does not address these issues may be inadequate for those with dual diagnosis.

Treating the Addiction and Psychiatric Disorders with Medications

There are now many safe, nonaddicting medicines that can help ease the symptoms of emotional/psychiatric disorders, stabilize the mood, and increase the ability to concentrate on therapy. While a detailed description of the medications is beyond the scope of this text, the brief review that follows will introduce the basic concepts.

Medication Treatment for Affective Disorders (Depression or Mania)

Three classes of medications are used to help relieve the symptoms of bipolar disorder: mood stabilizers, atypical antipsychotics, and antidepressants.

- *Mood stabilizers*—The oldest and most common treatment for bipolar disorder is a nonaddicting mood stabilizer called lithium, which is actually a mineral mined from the earth. Although no one knows exactly how lithium helps to stabilize the mood swings of bipolar disorder, it is very effective. In the last ten to twenty years, other mood stabilizers that can enhance lithium's effectiveness have been discovered, including Depakote (generic name valproic acid), Neurontin (generic name gabapentin), Tegretol (generic name carbamazepine),

Trileptal (generic name oxcarbazepine), and Lamictal (generic name lamotrigine). All of these medications are nonaddicting, and many of them can also decrease cravings for alcohol and drugs.

- *Atypical antipsychotics*—This class of nonaddicting medications— which includes Seroquel (generic name quetiapine), Risperdal (generic name risperidone), Abilify (generic name aripiprazole), Zyprexa (generic name olanzapine) and Geodon (generic name ziprasidone)—is very effective in treating bipolar symptoms. In addition, these medications help to improve sleep and decrease anxiety, while some may also help relieve certain components of major depression. However, medications in this class slightly increase the risk of a serious side effect called tardive dyskinesia (repetitive, involuntary muscle movements in the limbs, face, and trunk). Be sure to ask your physician about this issue before using atypical antipsychotics.

- *Antidepressants*—Two classes of antidepressants may be help-ful: selective serotonin reuptake inhibitors (SSRIs) and selective norepinephrine reuptake inhibitors (SNRIs). The SSRIs—which include Lexapro (generic name escitalopram), Zoloft (generic name sertraline), and Paxil (generic name paroxetine hydrochloride)—can treat depression and bipolar disorder safely and effectively without the risk of addiction. They also exert some positive effects on al-coholism and drug addiction, although they are not considered treatments for these problems. The SNRIs—which include Effexor (generic name veniafaxine), Pristiq (generic name desvenlafaxine), and Cymbalta (generic name duloxetine)—have somewhat different mechanisms of action but achieve similar results.

All three of these classes of medications also reduce anxiety, which can help to decrease cravings and stabilize the major depression or bipolar disorder that brings about symptoms of anxiety.

Medication Treatment for Anxiety Disorders

Benzodiazepines such as Valium (generic name diazepam), Xanax (generic name alprazolam), and Ativan (generic name lorazepam) are very effective at reducing anxiety symptoms; however, people who are already struggling with addiction are at high risk of becoming addicted to these medications. Therefore, the benzodiazepines are *not* an option for patients with a dual diagnosis. Better options are some of the newer antidepressant medications and certain antiseizure and antipsychotic medicines, all of which can reduce anxiety without causing relapse. (See the discussion of medicines for affective disorders above for more information on these medications.)

Two other medications that seem to be quite effective for reducing anxiety are:

• Vistaril (generic name hydroxyzine)

• Desyrel (generic name trazodone)

Vistaril is similar to Benadryl, a familiar medicine found in many over-the-counter preparations for allergies, but it seems to have more of a focused, antianxiety effect. Trazodone is an older antidepressant that has been shown to have significant antianxiety effects plus the ability to induce sleep.

Family Education and Participation

Since family members often serve as caregivers, provide social and financial support, and are in a good position to monitor the recovering addict's progress, it is important that they be included in the treatment program. A spouse or significant other, parents, siblings, and children can all play positive roles in the recovery and—at the very least—can learn to protect themselves from the combination of addiction and psychiatric disease.

Families can do much to help their loved ones and themselves by realizing that substance dependence and psychiatric illness are diseases that require treatment. They need to understand that they *cannot* stop the addicted person's substance dependence but *must* stop making it easy for him or her to continue practicing the addiction and living in denial. When dealing with someone with a dual diagnosis, it's easy for family members to develop their own dysfunctional coping skills. Therefore, learning to cope in healthy, life-affirming ways is a must. (Be sure to review the concepts in Chapter Eight.)

The family also needs to ensure that the addicted person gets well-coordinated dual diagnosis treatment. If this is not readily available, the family should enroll him or her in two separate programs (mental health and addiction treatment). In many cases, these two programs can be coordinated by applying the concepts outlined in this chapter. The family can also be of great help in facilitating communication between the two programs.

The good news is that, when given proper treatment, people with a dual diagnosis have a strong chance of achieving sobriety and good mental health. So family members should take heart: these dual diseases are very treatable.

The Dual Diagnosis 12-Step Program: Dual Recovery Anonymous

A 12-step program is an essential part of the dual diagnosis treatment. Dual Recovery Anonymous (DRA) is a program and support group based on the 12-step program utilized by Alcoholics Anonymous (AA) and Narcotics Anonymous (NA). While it is fine for those with dual diagnoses to attend regular 12-step meetings (such as AA or NA), DRA focuses specifically on issues related to dual diagnosis and therefore may be more helpful. Dual Recovery Anonymous groups emphasize the importance of treating the addiction and the psychiatric disorder simultaneously and consistently. The program encourages the responsible use of psychiatric medications, teaches healthy coping skills, and helps members develop new, sober social networks. Some of my patients go to both AA and DRA: they have a "home group" in each program and split their attendance between the two. However, if a DRA group is not available, either AA or NA is an excellent adjunct to a dual diagnosis treatment program.

A Note on Caffeine and Sleep

All those undergoing treatment for addiction or psychiatric illness should decrease the use of caffeine significantly, especially during the withdrawal and "post-acute" withdrawal phases, or in cases of an anxiety or a mood disorder.

Although caffeine is only a mild stimulant for most people, high doses can make some people feel jittery or on edge and may interfere with sleep. People generally develop tolerance to caffeine's stimulating effects after using it for only about two to three weeks, but do *not* develop much of a tolerance to its anxiety or irritability provoking and sleep disruption effects.

Most of caffeine's stimulating effects are psychological, not physiological. In other words, just seeing the coffee pot or coffee shop, smelling the aroma, feeling the heat, adding your particular combination of cream and sugar, all cause you to "feel stimulated." (If you really wanted to use it as a stimulant, you would need to increase your dose every two to three weeks. After about six months, you would have to drink a pot and a half of coffee if you really wanted it to wake you up. If you switch to decaf beverages—which have some caffeine but very little compared to caffeinated ones—prepare them the same way, and drink them in the same environments, you will probably achieve your morning eye-opener without caffeine.)

Caffeine can be a significant problem for addicts or those with dual diagnosis in recovery, for they tend to become exquisitely sensitive to it—so much so that a cup of coffee on Monday morning can still be causing sleep problems or irritability on Thursday evening!

Tapering Off

It is important to deal with this issue by slowly tapering off of caffeinated beverages and switching to decaffeinated ones. I am not asking you to give up caffeine for the rest of your life, just to stop all caffeine for one month and see if any of the problems associated with its consumption—such as difficulty sleeping, excessive anxiety or nervousness, or irritability—go away. If you do not notice any changes for the better, slowly add caffeine back to your diet and see if you notice any negative changes recurring.

Start out with the amount of caffeine that you usually ingest, and cut it in half every two days, until you are off of it. Suppose, for example, that you drink four cups of coffee each day. Switch to two cups of regular and two cups of decaf for two days, then one cup of regular and three cups of decaf for two days, then half a cup of regular mixed with half a cup of decaf (sometimes called "half-caf") and three cups of decaf for two days. After that, just drink decaf. We usually get caffeine in three beverage forms—coffee, sodas, and iced tea—and you want to be drinking only the decaf forms of all three. Iced tea can be a problem in restaurants, for you have no way of knowing if they are really giving you the decaf version. I strongly recommend that when you are trying to stay off caffeine, you do not order iced tea outside of your home. Instead, make a big pitcher of decaf tea at home, and only drink it there.

Sleep

Both addiction and psychiatric disorders can interfere with sleep. Sleep is a very important part of a healthy lifestyle, and it is vital for recovery. (If you have problems sleeping, you will be more tired and irritable. This will make you more anxious and more easily upset, which, in turn, will increase the odds you'll misinterpret these feelings as cravings for alcohol or drugs, thereby increasing your chances for a relapse.) If you can sleep at least a restful seven hours a night—eight to nine hours is better for most people—you have a much better chance of remaining sober and keeping your psychiatric illness in check.

The solution to sleep problems associated with addiction is multifaceted, and it includes increasing your daily exercise, eating healthfully, and practicing stress management and relaxation techniques (especially visualization, deep breathing, and deep muscle relaxation exercises). As for medications, members of the benzodiazepine class are off limits because they can become addicting: Halcion, Lunesta, and Restoril are not options for addicts, alcoholics, or dual diagnosis patients. Vistaril (hydroxyzine) and trazodone are effective and safe enough to be used as sleep aids. Some of the newer atypical antipsychotics such as Seroquel, Zyprexa, or Rispirdal, in low doses, are also very effective.

A Few Final Words

Recovery from addiction is difficult, to say the least. For those who also suffer from an emotional or psychiatric illness, it's an even greater challenge. The good news is that most people with dual disorders *are* able to regain their health and emotional stability and lead productive lives, especially when they receive integrated dual diagnosis treatment—combined psychiatric and substance dependence treatment from the same clinician or treatment team. When only half of the dual diagnosis is treated, symptoms may continue to linger. But with effective, integrated treatment, there is hope!

Key Points Review

- A person who has both an addiction and a psychiatric disorder is said to have a dual diagnosis.

- Not only is the person with a dual diagnosis affected by two distinct illnesses (addiction and psychiatric disorder), each makes the other worse, which complicates recovery.

- The psychiatric disorders that often accompany addiction include mood disorders (major depression, mania, bipolar disease), anxiety disorders, and psychotic disorders (schizophrenia or schizoaffective disorders).

- To recover fully, a person with a dual diagnosis must receive comprehensive treatment for both problems simultaneously.

- Comprehensive treatment for the dual diagnosis includes treatment for the addiction, treatment for the psychiatric illness, participation in a 12-step program, appropriate nonaddicting medication for each illness, and family education and participation for both illnesses.

- Family members need to realize that they cannot stop the addicted person's substance dependence but must stop making it easy for him or her to continue practicing the addiction and living in denial.

- A 12-step program called Dual Recovery Anonymous, based on the 12-step program developed by Alcoholics Anonymous, can be an integral part of dual diagnosis recovery.

- I highly recommend that you taper off all caffeine for at least one month at the beginning of your sobriety in order to reduce insomnia, anxiety, and irritability.

- Addressing any sleep problems with your physician early in recovery is essential for treatment success.

CHAPTER EIGHT

The Recovering Family

"I am so tired of trying to handle the family responsibilities, the finances and everything else all by myself."

"My kids hate their Dad for disappointing them so many times. Can you really blame them?"

"She's not trying hard enough to stay away from her drug buddies."

"If he really cared about us, he wouldn't have blown all our savings... again!"

"If he shows his face here again, I will kick him out before he gets through the front door."

"She doesn't even remember slapping the kids around! How can she not remember?"

"I went to some stupid counseling session with him. The idiot shrink told me I was an enabler and insinuated that this disease had affected me as well."

I've heard many comments like these from the families of my patients, and they illustrate a sad truth: addiction is never just one person's problem—it devastates entire families. When your family member is in the throes of addiction, you can feel abandoned, anxious, fearful, angry, embarrassed, guilty, and a host of other emotions. The damage extends throughout the entire family as you struggle to cover up the problem, work around the addict, deal with your own negative emotions, and cope with the responsibilities the addict left untended and the roles that are unfulfilled. You, the family members, often become enablers unwittingly, helping the addict continue his or her damaging behavior and keeping the addiction in play. For all of these reasons, you need to be in recovery right along with the addict, although you may not realize that you need help.

The most important thing for you, the family member of an addict, to understand is that addiction is a disease, not a moral failing or inborn sin. That's a good thing, because the disease of addiction is treatable and manageable with appropriate medical assistance, while sin is not. It may be difficult to arrive at this new understanding, and you may have trouble letting go of years of accumulated anger and resentment, but always remember that your new understanding and skills will help your addicted loved one recover—and will help improve your life tremendously.

In this chapter, I look at the effects of addiction recovery on the addicted person's family and explain how family members can work together to support each other through this difficult process.

Defining the Family

In days past, when we spoke about a "family," we typically meant Mom, Dad, and the kids, plus possibly some grandparents and an aunt or uncle. Today, the definition of "family" is much broader and includes people living together who aren't married, a single person with children, a gay or straight married couple, three generations that live together in one household, and people unrelated by blood or marriage who share a household, among other combinations and arrangements. Generally speaking, people living together in a household and related to each other by blood are considered immediate family; if they're not related by blood, they're still considered to be a family.

Family members are sometimes geographically dispersed due to marital separation and divorce. In some cases, parents of a child or children may never have lived under the same roof. Blended families, a combination of two families resulting from divorce or death of a spouse followed by remarriage, are becoming more and more common these days. In short, there are many ways to define a family. But no matter which form a family takes, each member needs to be loved and cared for, and each is affected by another member's addiction.

How Addiction Harms the Family

John, a forty-seven-year-old real estate appraiser, had been a heavy drinker since his teenage years. But after suffering a substantial financial reversal, his drinking escalated. Angry rants at home after several drinks became a nightly debacle. He repeatedly chose the dinner hour to vent his rage against the world in general and his family in particular. His wife and two daughters soon learned to act as if they barely noticed that he yelled at them for no real reason and threw his chair against the wall before stomping away from the dinner table, leaving the meal uneaten. They continued to try to have a pleasant dinner conversation, although it was repeatedly interrupted by rude comments yelled by John from the other room. In truth, the bland, "we don't notice" attitude that John's wife and daughters adopted was simply a ruse—underneath it all, their stomachs churned and their hearts pounded. Eventually one of the girls developed an alcohol problem of her own, while the other developed an eating disorder.

This story is not unusual. Family members can and do suffer from a variety of problems related to their loved one's addiction. These include:

• physical, emotional, and sexual abuse (as victim or perpetrator)

• difficulty in managing anger

• poor self-esteem

- anxiety disorders

- depression

- frequent medical illnesses

- difficulty in forming and maintaining relationships

- marital problems or divorce

- their own addictions

And it's not just the immediate family, or the family members living with the addict, who are affected. It doesn't matter if a son lives fifty miles away and only sees his addicted mother on weekends, or if a sister sees her addicted brother only once a year. When an addict is part of a nuclear, immediate, or extended family, or part of any family arrangement, the consequences of his or her behavior will be felt by everyone. That's why family members, especially those living with the addict, need treatment, although a different kind than that provided to the addict. Family members need to learn how to recognize the problems caused by the addiction, understand the roles they have unwittingly played in the addiction, assess the psychological damage they have suffered, and develop new interpersonal skills. The good news is that much of the harm that addiction causes family members is reversible with the proper treatment.

Issues for Families of Addicts

Families have new coping and communications skills to master as they learn to protect themselves from the poison of their loved one's addiction, and to support him or her through the recovery process. In a sense, they are also in recovery, and *it is just as important for them to "graduate" successfully from treatment as it is for the addict.*

In the sections that follow, we'll look at the emotional toll addiction takes on the family, as well as codependency, addiction's impact on children, and the question of physical and sexual abuse.

The Emotional Toll Taken on the Family

In a healthy, well-functioning family, all members feel free to communicate with one another, express their emotions, trust each other, and tell the truth. But this is simply not the case in most families of addicts. Instead, family members develop attitudes and behaviors, such as denial, low self-esteem, compliance, and desire for control, that help them survive emotionally—but certainly not thrive.

Family Members' Quiz

The following quiz is for family members of an addict. How many of these feelings, thoughts, and behaviors do you have? Place a check mark next to the sentences that apply to you.

Denial

____ I deny my own needs and feelings in the name of being unselfish and dedicated to the well-being of others.

____ I have a difficult time knowing what I feel.

____ I deny, change, or minimize how I truly feel.

Low Self-Esteem

____ I value others' approval of my feelings, actions, and thinking over my own.

____ I do not see myself as a worthwhile or lovable person.

____ I have a hard time making decisions.

____ I think just about everything I say, do or think is "not good enough."

____ I feel self-conscious when I receive positive strokes or gifts from others.

_____ I do not speak up for myself or ask others to honor my needs or desires.

Compliance

_____ I am afraid to express my own opinions and feelings, especially if they are different from those of others.

_____ I ignore my own interests and desires in order to do what others want.

_____ I offer sex when I want love.

_____ I am so loyal that I'd rather stay in a destructive situation than leave.

_____ I value the opinions and feelings of others more than my own.

_____ To avoid making others angry and possibly rejecting me, I submerge my own values and integrity.

Control

_____ I become resentful when others refuse my help.

_____ I use sex to get acceptance and approval.

_____ I freely offer suggestions and advice to others without being asked.

_____ I must feel that I'm needed before I can have a relationship with another person.

_____ I go overboard in bestowing favors and gifts on the people I care about.

_____ I believe most other people are not capable of taking care of themselves.

_____ I try to persuade others to think and feel the way I think they should.

Many people exhibit these feelings, thoughts, and behaviors. However, if you've checked off eight or more items, you are probably suffering from a great deal of emotional distress that is most likely related to the addiction in the family. The first step toward recovery is recognition of the problem: only then can you begin taking steps to heal it.

Codependency

One of the major problems seen in the families of addicts is codependency, a complex relationship between the addict and a family member (or, in some cases, friend) that appears to be loving but is actually dangerous and damaging to all involved.

Codependency is a habitual pattern of self-defeating coping mechanisms. The codependent offers help to the addict, but it's too much help and is often inappropriate. The addict learns to depend on the codependent to help "fix" his or her problems. For example, the codependent may give the addict money or a place to live, bail him or her out of jail, call in excuses to the boss, smooth things over with other family members when the addict "misbehaves," and otherwise clean up the addict's messes. Because the codependent protects the addict from the negative consequences of the addiction, the addict can continue drinking or using (sometimes we say that the family member is "enabling" the addict to keep using). Codependent behavior can be active, as in giving the addicted son a new car after he got loaded and smashed up the old one. It can also be passive, as in pretending not to notice that Mom is usually drunk and makes crude or rude comments at dinner parties and other social outings.

Paul's wife, Linda, had been drinking alcohol daily for over four years. He had begged her to stop countless times, and every "morning after" she swore that she would quit, but she never seemed to get around to it. At least part of the reason may have been that Paul unwittingly made it easy for Linda to continue drinking. When she couldn't seem to handle her responsibilities at home, he hired a housekeeper and brought home takeout for dinner. When she was arrested for driving under the influence, he bailed her out of jail immediately.

So you can see that codependence is a set of dysfunctional behaviors that family members adopt in order to survive the emotional pain and stress caused by the addiction. For example, a woman with a husband who is addicted to cocaine may end up raising her children virtually on her own. The fact that Daddy never makes it to school events, doesn't participate in child care activities, and lost his job because he can't get up in the morning is never mentioned. Other dysfunctional behaviors include children taking on adult responsibilities, families sharply curtailing social activities so no one will see the addiction behavior, and family members denying their own needs because the addict is incapable of providing for them.

These enabling behaviors may temporarily lessen conflict and ease tension within the family, but in the long run they are counterproductive. They protect the addict from negative consequences and "grant permission" for the continuation of destructive behavior. While each family member may suppress or deny their angry or uncomfortable feelings about both the addict and the situation, these feelings don't disappear. Often they reemerge in the form of:

- depression
- outbursts of rage
- controlling behavior
- distrust
- perfectionism
- avoidance of feelings (especially those linked to the stress and emotional pain the addict causes)
- problems with intimacy
- excessive caretaking
- physical illness related to stress

Addiction's Impact on Children

Ten-year-old Laurie had spent most of her childhood coping with a mother who had a severe alcohol problem. Laurie, who didn't have a father, learned early on how to do the grocery shopping, clean the house, and cook a meal, since more often than not, these chores fell to her. Laurie's mother was in no condition to help her with her homework, so Laurie struggled with her studies alone. Her clothes were usually old, ill fitting, or inappropriate because her mother hardly ever shopped for her. In spite of all of this, Laurie decided to celebrate her tenth birthday by having a slumber party, with her mother's permission. But when her mother made a drunken appearance at the party, Laurie was so mortified that she never invited anyone to her house again. However, she never said anything to her mother about the incident, as she was afraid it might trigger an even bigger binge.

Although addiction takes many forms and may play out in different ways, one thing is certain: it always takes an emotional toll on the addict's children. Even if a child is no longer living with a substance-abusing parent, because of separation, divorce, abandonment, incarceration, or death, that child will still suffer. And if the child does not get treatment, the deleterious effects of the addiction can continue even if the parent is no longer actively drinking or using.

In families where alcohol or drugs are abused, parental behavior is frequently unpredictable and communication is unclear. Family life is characterized by chaos and volatility. One moment a parent may be loving and engaged, the next withdrawn, illogical, or downright "crazy." Structure and rules may be rigid, inconsistent, nonexistent, or a combination of all three. Not understanding that a parent's behavior and mood is determined by the amount of alcohol or other drugs recently ingested, a child may justifiably feel confused and insecure. While he may love and feel concern for his parent, he may also feel angry and hurt that the parent does not love him enough to stop using. As a result, the child of an addict can adopt abnormal coping skills that, in turn, may result in:

- depression

- withdrawal

- anger

- isolation

- low self-esteem

- insomnia or excessive sleeping

- behavioral problems such as irritability, hyperactivity, disruptive behavior, vandalism

- difficulties at school, including tardiness, excessive absence, lack of concentration, poor study habits, fluctuating performance

- caretaking of the addict or of other children in the family who have been neglected by the addict

- disheveled, unkempt, or otherwise inappropriate appearance, due to neglect of the abusing parent (Monday is often a "sloppy day" due to the parent's substance use on the weekend)

- exhaustion due to parental late-night arguing or violent behavior

- unexplained bruises or burns due to lack of parental supervision or physical abuse by the addicted parent

- talking about violent or abusive situations at home

- stomachaches, headaches, or other physical ailments with no apparent cause, which often arise at the same time every day as the child thinks about having to go home soon

- rejection by peers who know about the substance-abusing parent

Many children blame themselves for their parent's rages or even for their substance dependence. They believe it when a parent screams at them for being stupid or lazy, or insists that he or she wouldn't drink or use so much if the children stopped fighting, kept their rooms clean, or got better grades. Some children try to control the abuse or habitual use by getting straight As, keeping the house spic and span, or getting along perfectly with their siblings. Others withdraw, hoping not to create any disturbance that might cause an outburst or a binge. Without counseling, few children realize that the rages are actually the result of drug or alcohol abuse, not their own failings. They don't know that they cannot control the parent's behavior or cure the addiction by acting a certain way, any more than they can cure a parent's heart disease or diabetes.

The children of addicts are often frightened, and with good reason. Alcohol and drug abuse go hand in hand with domestic violence, so there is a good chance that these children may witness or be the victims of violence or physical or sexual abuse. As a result, the children of addicts can suffer from post-traumatic stress syndrome, experiencing the same kinds of sleep disturbances, flashbacks, anxiety, and depression suffered by soldiers. Not only are they frightened for their own well-being, they also harbor the all-too-real fear that the addicted parent may get sick or die as a result of the drinking or drug use.

Despite the fact that friends can be buffers offering relief from problems at home, many children of addicts have a limited social life. They may avoid bringing friends home or appearing with the family in public, because of the addicted parent's inappropriate behaviors. They may shy away from making friends at all, because they're afraid someone will find out how bizarre their life really is. Making matters worse, other parents may warn their children to stay away from these youngsters because of their troubled families, limiting their social circles even further.

On the other hand, some children of addicts use friends as buffers and use their leadership skills to earn key positions in school and extracurricular activities, which means they can spend less time at home. These children appear to be well-adjusted high achievers, but often their considerable accomplishments don't assuage their deep-seated fears.

The effects of a parent's alcohol or drug addiction visit deep, long-lasting, and far-reaching consequences on their children. In fact, long after a child has grown up and left the home, problems can continue to manifest. The adult child of an addict may, for example, be afraid to trust a spouse or partner who stops for a drink with friends after work, thinking this behavior might turn into an addiction. There may be a lingering fear of being abandoned or abused that interferes with close personal relationships. (This is especially true if the spouse or partner is the same gender as the abusing parent.) There may be a strong need to control the behavior of a spouse or partner and other family members in an attempt to avoid the dysfunction and chaotic behavior of his or her early family life.

Fortunately, the children of addicts do not have to repeat the dysfunctional behavior patterns of the past. With proper treatment, these adult children can acquire healthy coping skills that can lead to rewarding interpersonal relationships and a satisfying family life.

Abuse Issues in Addicted Families

Physical and sexual abuse are ever-present threats to the children of addicts, with both occurring frequently in chaotic and dysfunctional families in which communication has broken down and roles are blurred. Even if a child is not the target of abuse, he or she is six times more likely to witness spousal abuse than other children, which in itself has emotionally destructive consequences.

Children who come from high-conflict homes tend to have lower self-esteem than others and believe that their destinies are controlled by external forces such as fate, God, or other powerful entities. As a result, they are less likely to stand up for themselves and will accept just about any kind of attention (including negative or abusive attention), which greatly increases the risk that they will be victimized in the future. Female children of alcoholics, in particular, are more likely to be involved with men who abuse alcohol or drugs, increasing their likelihood of being abused as adults.

As a result of these and other stressors, children of addicts often have difficulty in school. They may be unable to focus on their schoolwork or complete their homework, because of the conflicts and tensions at home. They are also more likely than their peers to have learning disabilities, be truant, repeat grades, transfer schools, and be expelled.

These children may also be harmed in other ways. For example, they will suffer from an economic downturn when a parent loses a job because of drinking or drug use. They may develop stress-related ailments such as gastrointestinal disorders, headaches, migraines, or asthma. Regular doctor and dentist visits may be ignored, and immunizations and other routine medical care forgotten. And they might be injured if an addicted parent neglects to provide proper supervision, child-proof the house, or attend to the children's everyday needs.

The sad truth is that one in four children of addicts become addicts themselves. However, most of these children do manage to cope with their circumstances and succeed in life. It is certainly possible for them to learn to develop their inner strength and draw on it. Al-Anon (or Alateen, for younger people) is a 12-step group specifically formed for those who have been affected by someone else's substance abuse. It's a good place to start to find "solutions that lead to serenity." Al-Anon and Alateen can help family members find a better way of life and discover happiness, whether or not the addict is still drinking or abusing.

The Benefits of Family Therapy

Spouses, children, siblings, parents, and others—*everyone in the family suffers when one is an addict, and the problems can be severe and long lasting*. Fortunately, families do *not* have to remain in the grip of alcohol or drugs; once a family realizes that it is in crisis, its members can find help. There are several therapeutic approaches that can help turn a family around and put it on the path toward recovery and a healthy lifestyle. Some steps in family therapy include:

- *Attaining sobriety*—Initially, the main focus should be to encourage the addict to get into treatment. A counselor can help the family set up an effective intervention.

- *Adjusting to sobriety*—It's a must to shake off old habits and develop new family roles, rules, and relationships based on mutual trust. This includes opening up communication channels between family members and allowing everyone to say what they think without worrying about setting off a lapse or relapse in the addict. It also includes holding the addict responsible for his behavior. Doing all of these will require developing new coping skills to deal with stressful situations, learning to communicate openly, taking care of oneself and one's own needs, eating well and exercising often, and practicing stress management techniques such as yoga or meditation.

- *Maintaining sobriety in the long run*—Developing and practicing healthy family habits will encourage the addict to remain sober and help the family maintain its equilibrium even if the addict returns to drinking or using.

Once positive changes are in motion, the individual and family recovery processes generally parallel each other, although they may not work in perfect harmony. Should lapse or relapse occur, it is more important than ever that family members continue to practice their own new healthy behaviors. These healthy new habits can actually *help to stop a lapse or relapse* in progress.

Healthy Problem-Solving Skills

One of the keys to successful family functioning is the development and usage of healthy problem-solving skills. In families of addicts, problems are typically ignored or covered up. But in recovering families, the problems must be addressed and solved in an open, healthy manner. For example:

Problem Solving

Situation	Past Practice	New Skill
Dad passes out drunk at the dinner table.	Ignore him. Talk about what happened at school, the weather or anything else, but don't mention what happened.	Everyone leaves the table and gathers elsewhere to plan what the family will do if Dad does not go into treatment immediately. Confront Dad the next morning when he is sober.
Mom spends the food allowance on drugs.	The family borrows money from Uncle John (yet again) just so they can eat.	Mom is not allowed to have any access to money, so that the family can be assured that they can always buy food, while paying back Uncle John.
Teenage daughter is suspended for getting high at school.	Parents confront her. She blames the incident on friends and promises never to do it again.	Daughter is grounded for a month and taken to a counselor who specializes in evaluation for addiction.
Teenage son is arrested for drunk driving.	Parents bail him out of jail and pay a high-priced lawyer to get him off. He is grounded for a weekend and then gets his car back.	Son is left in jail overnight. He gets very scared in jail and becomes willing to do whatever it takes to avoid repeating the experience. He is enrolled in a treatment program right after his release from jail.

In order to master these habits, each family member will need to adopt a new set of attitudes, thoughts, and communication skills that includes the following:

- I do not expect others to read my mind.
- I will not let hurts and problems build up. I will address them as quickly as possible.
- I will stop and think before expressing irritation.
- I will give constructive (not destructive) criticism.
- I will address specific behavior, not personal attributes.
- I will express any criticism in terms of my own feelings.
- I will request specific behavior changes.
- I will offer to compromise.
- I will express my positive feelings.
- I will mean what I say and say what I mean.
- I will learn and practice healthy new strategies to calm down.

To ensure clear communication and effective problem solving, family roles and rules must be clear yet be somewhat flexible to allow for the changes that are bound to happen in everyday living. The parents must hold the power in the family, not the children; while children are respected, they have considerably less authority. Individual family members should be able to reduce their personal stress by calling on others for support, understanding, and assistance. Change should proceed at a pace that allows for healthy adaptation of new coping skills by all the members.

The goal is to rebuild a healthy, functional family in which all members feel free to express their emotions, talk with one another, trust one another, and tell the truth. In most families, some form of external therapy (counselor, Al-Anon) will be required to make these changes successfully.

The Lapse/Relapse Consequences Agreement

At some point in most addiction treatment programs, the therapist will ask the addict and family to draw up a Lapse/Relapse Consequences Agreement, which spells out for the addict the consequences of sliding back into substance use.

One of the reasons that addicts continue to drink or use is they are in denial about the addiction. It's easy to perpetuate this denial when family members and friends protect addicts from the consequences of their harmful behavior. But once in treatment, it's important for addicts to understand that any lapse or relapse will harm them and their families, and that they will need to face the consequences of such actions.

That's where the Lapse/Relapse Consequences Agreement comes in. This written document spells out an agreement between the addict and another person, usually a spouse or significant other, parent, sibling, child, or friend. The agreement is signed, and both parties keep a copy so there can be no disagreement over the consequences. This agreement is not just for the addict; it's for both parties, each of whom is encouraged to break away from the old roles of addict and victim/enabler. This precludes denial in the addict and helps the family member or friend regain some control.

Working together, the two parties will draw up a list of consequences (punishments) for each lapse or relapse. The consequences should be serious and unpleasant but not so onerous that they destroy relationships or the chance of reestablishing a healthy and happy life. For example, one consequence may be that the addict has to move out of the house for three days, during which time she must go to six AA meetings, meet with her sponsor three times, document these activities, and have them signed off on a piece of paper by the individuals involved, before they are allowed to return home.

The Lapse/Relapse Consequences Agreement shouldn't be considered an academic exercise: drawing up the agreement and abiding by it forces everyone to face reality. The addict will experience the consequences of his or her actions with every single lapse or relapse, and family members and friends will see that demanding consequences can help them as much as it helps the addict.

Here is a Lapse/Relapse Consequences Agreement between Jeanette and her husband, Jeremy.

Jeanette's Lapse/Relapse Consequences Agreement

The behavior to be avoided: _Drinking any amount of alcohol at all._

First lapse consequences: _Attend three extra AA meetings in five day. Jeanette is also not allowed to stay at the house or see her children for those five days. She must meet with her AA sponsor daily for as long as the sponsor deems appropriate._

Second lapse consequences: _Jeanette must return immediately to her intensive outpatient treatment program and complete the program all over again. She must attend AA daily for thirty days and is not allowed to stay at the house or see the children for ten days. She must follow all of her sponsor's directives and recommendations to prevent further relapse. She must also see her addiction psychiatrist and agree to all recommendations for medication._

Third lapse consequences: _Jeanette must add individual counseling for addiction issues to her current addiction treatment program. She must attend ninety meetings in ninety days_

and meet with her sponsor daily for thirty days and follow all
of her recommendations. She is not allowed to stay at the house
see her children for 15 days. She agrees to add Antabuse to her
medication regimen if her physician recommends it. She also
agrees to let Jeremy watch her take her Antabuse every day.

Signed by: _____ Jeanette _____   _____ Jeremy _____

Now try drawing up your own Lapse/Relapse Consequences
Agreement. Make several copies of the blank form below. Then fill it out,
and update it regularly.

Lapse/Relapse Consequences Agreement Worksheet

The behavior to be avoided: _____

_____

_____

First lapse consequences:_____

_____

_____

Second lapse consequences: _____

_____

_____

Signed by: _____   _____

You can find printable copies of the Lapse/Relapse Consequences Agreement on www.EnterHealth.com/ HealingtheAddictedBrain.

Getting Help

The counselors at any addiction treatment center can recommend individual therapists, family therapists, and groups that offer help to the addicted person and his or her family and friends. Individual therapists typically focus on specific issues of sobriety and teach the addict new, more effective ways to deal with stress. Sometimes they will also address family issues. Family therapists typically engage all family members to help identify unhealthy patterns of behavior in the family and replace them with new, healthier patterns. Group therapy typically involves multiple families at the same time, so that families can share ideas about and solutions to their mutual problems, while providing support for each other. Many times, the family can benefit from a combination of these different therapy styles.

In addition to individual, family, and group counseling, there are organizations that specialize in treating family members. These include:

- *Al-Anon*—Founded by the wife of the man who established Alcoholics Anonymous, Al-Anon is a 12-step group offering support to the family and friends of addicts. Participants are taught to recognize the addiction-encouraging behaviors that exist in their families, identify them as part of the disease process, understand that they have been harmed by the disease, and to forgive both the addict and themselves.

- *Alateen*—Another 12-step group, Alateen is basically Al-Anon aimed at teenagers (aged twelve through twenty). This age group may be in need of more support than any other because they are going through a stressful, constantly changing phase of life.

Add an addicted family member to the mix, and things can get really tough.

- *Nar-Anon*—A 12-step program designed for the family and friends of drug addicts, similar to Al-Anon.

- *Betty Ford Children's Program*—The Betty Ford Center has developed an excellent treatment program aimed at children ages 7-12 years of age. Unfortunately it is only offered in a few cities throughout the U.S. Go to www.bettyfordcenter.org/children for further information.

- At www.EnterHealth.com/HealingtheAddictedBrain you can find specific information for family therapy and family members can learn almost all of the concepts that an addict learns in treatment (*i.e.*, cravings, triggers, etc.), so both parties are working with the same information. This information is immensely helpful for family members, because so often they have very little understanding of what is being taught in treatment sessions. Although it is very similar to what you are learning in this book, it is much more comprehensive.

Curing the "Family Curse"

Addiction has a very strong genetic component: the children of an addict have at least a fifty-fifty chance of becoming addicts themselves. However, genetic tendency only indicates a risk. Those who never use alcohol or drugs cannot become addicted. Therefore, it's extremely important that the children of alcoholics and the children of substance abusers learn that abstention is the best prevention.

It's important to note that alcoholism and drug dependence sometimes skips generations. This may be because children of alcoholics and addicts witness firsthand the effects of addiction on the addict and the family and choose not to drink or use drugs at all. However, their own children—who may have inherited the same genetic susceptibility toward addiction that ensnared their grandparent—don't know what it's like to live with an addict and don't fear addiction the way their parents did. Thus, the grandchildren can more easily slip into addiction if they begin drinking or using.

The best way to prevent this is for both the addicted grandparents and the parents to have continued, open, and honest discussions with the grandchildren, beginning when they are young. Without exaggerating or sensationalizing, the parents and grandparents should lay out the facts and make it clear to the grandchildren that they may have inherited a genetic tendency to develop a serious, sometimes fatal disease, and that the best way to prevent it is to stay away from alcohol and drugs completely.

Not for Addicts Only

Once sixteen-year-old Gina's mother was firmly established in individual counseling for her alcohol addiction, Gina was asked to play a part in the treatment, which included going to Alateen. At first Gina was very pleasant and cooperative, but after about a week she started canceling meetings and refusing to go to Alateen. She grew very angry whenever the treatment team tried to involve her in her mother's therapy. "Why should I have to spend so much of my summer vacation humoring my mom and everybody else? I want to be with my friends and have some fun! It's my mother's problem, not mine! Give me a break!"

Yes, having to go to therapy or to Al-Anon or Alateen because someone else in the family is addicted can feel like a real burden. Many family members have asked me, "Why do *I* have to go through all this crap for them?! *They* screwed up, not me!" The answer is that the family members should do it for themselves. They've spent years living with and for the addict. They probably have no idea how their own behavior has encouraged and perpetuated the problem and made life harder for everyone (including themselves). Now it's time for the family members to examine their own actions and take care of their own mental and physical health.

If you're a family member, remember that family therapy may be the greatest gift you have ever given yourself. A well thought-through plan of action that will reduce or eliminate the stress, chaos, and unhappiness that comes from loving an addicted person.

All Therapists Are Not Alike

Whether you are wrestling with an addiction or you simply love someone with this problem, the importance of getting good therapy cannot be overstated. Ideally, the individual, family, or group therapist that you work with will deal with your specific issues sensitively and skillfully. Unfortunately, even knowledgeable and experienced therapists may drop the ball at times, or simply not be a good fit. If that happens, please do not use the unsatisfactory experience as an excuse to drop out of therapy. Yes, bad therapy can be a miserable experience, dashing your hopes and wasting time and money. But good therapy is absolutely necessary! If it doesn't work with the first therapist, look for another. Addiction is life-threatening for the addict and sanity-threatening for the family. Therapy works, and it's vital. Keep looking until you find someone who can help you.

Key Points Review

- Addiction is never just one person's problem; it devastates entire families.

- Families of addicts struggle to cover up the problem, work around the addict, deal with their own negative emotions, and cope with the addict's untended responsibilities and unfulfilled roles.

- Family members often unwittingly become enablers, helping

the addict to continue his or her damaging behavior and keep the addiction in play.

- Family members can suffer from addiction-related problems, including physical, emotional, and sexual abuse, difficulty in managing anger, poor self-esteem, anxiety, depression, frequent illnesses, relationship difficulties, and divorce.

- Parents' alcohol or drug addictions can cause deep, long-lasting, and far-reaching problems for their children.

- Many children blame themselves for their parent's alcohol- or drug-induced rages, or even for the parent's substance dependence problem.

- Like the addict, the family must also go through a recovery process.

- If they receive the proper treatment, the children of addicts will not have to repeat the dysfunctional behavior patterns of the past.

- In families of an addict, problems are typically ignored or covered up. In the recovering family, they must be addressed and solved in an open, healthy manner.

- The Lapse/Relapse Consequences Agreement is a contract between the addict and a significant other. Together, the two parties draw up a list of consequences (punishments) for any backward slide into addiction behaviors.

- Help for the families of addicts can come in the form of individual therapy, family therapy, or group therapy.

- Organizations that specialize in helping family members of addicts include Al-Anon, Alateen, and Nar-Anon, the Betty Ford Children's program, and www.EnterHealth.com/HealingtheAddictedBrain.

- Therapy works, and it's vital to the recovery of both the addict and his or her family. Keep looking until you find a therapist who can help.

CHAPTER NINE

Lapse and Relapse

Addicts don't suddenly start drinking or using again out of the blue. If you know what you're looking for, you can pick up subtle and not-so-subtle signs of danger in your behaviors. Even your thoughts can signal impending trouble. For example:

- Are you feeling so good about your recovery that you're getting overconfident?

- Are you under a lot of stress or having difficulty handling your emotions?

- Are you sending yourself discouraging, negative messages such as "I can't do this," "What's the point?" or "I might as well give up"?

- Are you withdrawing, even just a little, from your family and sober friends?

- Are you starting to hang out with some of your old drinking/using friends or going back to the same old drinking/using places?

- Are you ignoring your recovery process, hoping that it will take care of itself?

If you answered yes to any of those questions, you're in line for a lapse or relapse.

Lapses and relapses are common. But they don't begin when you reach for a bottle, light up a joint, or lay out a line. Lapsing or relapsing is a process that begins a long time before the actual event. Because lapses and relapses don't "just happen," it is possible to identify the signs of impending trouble and head it off. If you learn how to spot the warning signs, and make plans to act once you see them, you can stay on the road to recovery.

Lapse and Relapse—What's the Difference?

Lapse and relapse do not mean the same thing, even though the two words are often used interchangeably. A lapse is a slip; it's having one glass of wine at the dinner party, a single beer at a ball game, a joint at a party. A lapse is a brief episode of alcohol or drug use that does *not* signal a return to old usage habits and addictive patterns. You have that one glass of wine but do *not* call up your old drinking buddies and get smashed; you smoke that one joint but do *not* call your old dealer and begin keeping a stash again. Your head is *not* filled with thoughts of drinking or using after a lapse. Instead, you remain committed to your recovery.

A relapse, on the other hand, is a full-fledged dive back into old addictive thoughts and habits. You sip that single glass of wine at dinner; soon you're sneaking out for "just a few mouthfuls," thinking about how nice it would be to get blasted and party, drinking during the day at work and lying about it to your spouse at night, deliberately skipping AA or NA meetings, and so on.

There is a significant difference between a lapse and a relapse, but it's important to understand that they are points on the same continuum— and that continuum points in one direction only, the direction of danger. A lapse is *not* okay, and it is *not* better to suffer a bunch of "little lapses" rather than a single relapse. Neither is it true that a lapse can be ignored, while a relapse signals the end of all hope. Both lapses and relapses are warning signs that must be addressed immediately. With the right treatment, the problem can be corrected and even used as a basis for adjusting and improving your treatment program.

It's Worth Repeating...

I can't stress this point enough: neither lapses nor relapses can be ignored. Any time you drink or use, you are putting your health at risk and possibly endangering the lives of the people around you.

Always remember that suffering a lapse or relapse does *not* mean that you are a worthless weakling who will never get it right. Addiction is a chronic medical illness. Like asthma or diabetes, it is a lifelong disease that must be tended to and kept under control. People with diabetes sometimes lapse, neglecting to take their insulin and eating too much birthday cake. Those with high blood pressure may also lapse, ignoring their doctors' orders to take Lasix and gorging on salty food.

Anyone with a chronic medical illness may suffer a lapse or relapse, which should be viewed as part of the ups and downs of the disease process.

Anatomy of a Lapse or Relapse

A lapse or relapse does not begin when you down a beer or snort a line; that's just the "action phase" of the problem. Before that—often long before—the lapse or relapse takes root in your mind. It may start when sober life begins to feel too difficult to handle. For example, you may:

- experience upsetting or negative feelings such as anger, anxiety, boredom, depression, guilt, or loneliness
- have conflicts with the people with whom you socialize
- feel a lack of support from your friends or recovery network
- be forced to deal with problems you cannot solve
- feel really stressed out
- find it impossible to avoid running into some of your triggers

- feel strong cravings to use

- lose the structure (routine) of your daily life

- feel as if you'd love to celebrate something

- have to deal with an inadequately treated coexisting major psychiatric disorder such as major depression, in addition to your addiction

- suffer from physical pain the doctors can't relieve

- have to use prescription medicines that, even when properly prescribed and used, can get you high

- be forced to listen to alcohol- or drug-use stories (even at AA or NA meetings)

As one thought piles on top of another, the desire to drink or use may grow, pushing you closer to danger.

Perhaps your next step toward a lapse or relapse is a subtle shift in your attitude; you begin to feel like you have everything under control and don't see why you must continue with all the rules and restrictions. Or maybe your boss is giving you more and more work but you're afraid to ask for a breather because you don't want to look "weak." You may start to daydream a bit about getting high again, tell yourself that it's okay to skip some group meetings, or turn away from those annoying family members who always want you to "do the right thing." ("They just don't understand how hard it is to always do that darn right thing!") Maybe you take a few "little peeks" into your old world: driving by the bar where you used to drink, or having a friendly chat with your old drinking or drugging companions.

Andrea, an alcoholic, was responding well to addiction treatment that included the medication Antabuse (disulfiram). (Antabuse causes nausea, vomiting, and other unpleasant side effects when it mixes with alcohol in the body.) Andrea had agreed to take the Antabuse because she'd had a difficult time in the past staying sober. The plan was that

Jim, her husband, would give it to her each morning and watch her swallow it. During the first three weeks of treatment Andrea stayed completely sober and appeared to be on track. But then Jim had to go on a lengthy business trip. As soon as Jim told her about his upcoming business trip, Andrea began to fantasize about drinking. This fit right in with her old habit of drinking when she was alone, but she resisted the temptation. However, even though she had promised Jim she would continue to take the Antabuse while he was gone, she stopped after three days. "I'm doing fine," she told herself. "I don't need this." Then, two days later, Andrea had to take a brief plane trip in the morning to see her sick mother, and fly home the same day. This was a danger point, for Andrea had a history of drinking while on airplanes. Struggling to remain sober, she didn't actually drink on this trip—but she did purchase two small bottles of vodka. That night, alone in the house, she gave in and drank both bottles. Since there was still Antabuse in her system, she had an unpleasant reaction that sent her to the emergency room. She spent the next couple of days wondering whether or not she should tell Jim, and worrying about how he might react.

This is a key point: The lapse or relapse process is marked by predictable and identifiable warning signs that begin *long before* alcohol or drug use occurs. (In Andrea's case, as soon as Jim told her he was going on a business trip, the first warning sign appeared: she started fantasizing about drinking.) A lapse or relapse is inexorably propelled by powerful internal drives, the same ones that can make you drink from a poisoned well after days in the desert without water, or resort to cannibalism when you're stranded on a remote island with no other food sources. These drives defy logic and may sometimes gain added strength from an alcohol- or drug-addled cerebral cortex that encourages inaccurate thinking. The addict who suffers a lapse or relapse is not just being naughty: he or she is suffering from a serious disease that must be treated.

For a detailed list of people, places, ideas, and situations that might serve as triggers, see www.EnterHealth.com/ HealingtheAddictedBrain.

Signs of Impending Lapse or Relapse

The best way to handle lapse or relapse is prevention, which means learning to detect the signs of impending trouble early on and take steps immediately to stop the progression.

Fortunately, you can see the warning signs of imminent lapse or relapse as easily as you can see a fire truck's flashing red light. Generally speaking, the early signs are negative changes in attitudes, feelings, and behaviors. Below are nine warning signs of impending lapse or relapse, with examples of each. Some of these warning signs may seem innocuous and fairly common, as likely to strike non-addicts as easily and often as addicts: an increase in daily stress, disruption of the daily routine, neglecting healthy-living skills. (Doesn't almost everyone neglect *some* healthy-living skills?) Others may seem somewhat disturbing but not necessarily related to addiction: changes in behavior, withdrawing from family and (sober) friends, loss of judgment or control. It is possible to dismiss these as signs of stress or depression, but remember that stress and depression are also flash points for lapse and relapse. Then there are more serious warning signs, including going back into denial and suffering from delayed withdrawal symptoms.

Nine Warning Signs of Impending Lapse or Relapse

Let's look at nine warning signs to see if you are in danger of lapse or relapse. In the blank lines that follow each warning sign, make a note of your own personal issues. There are no right or wrong answers. The point is to alert you to the indications that a lapse or relapse is about to happen, and get you to think in advance about what might push you toward the edge.

1. Elevated stress from life events

You're super-stressed, a condition that may be related to:

- your family's lack of trust in you

- financial pressures caused by past addiction behaviors

- pressures at work caused by past addiction behaviors (such as absenteeism)

- missing your old drinking friends

- having to work harder to catch up on everything you avoided while using

- having no time to relax and have fun

What are the most stressful life events concerning *you* today?

_____

_____

_____

_____

2. Loss of daily structure

Your daily routine can be disrupted when you don't get enough sleep or you oversleep, skip meals, work late, miss work, or forget appointments. These things can happen for many reasons, including:

- vacations

- holidays

- a business trip

- a sick child

- a colleague at work is out sick, and you have to stay late to take up the slack

What is most likely to cause *you* to change your daily routine?

_____

_____

_____

_____

3. Neglecting healthy coping skills

You find yourself ignoring the skills you acquired in treatment and in 12-step programs, especially when you are stressed and really need them the most. Examples include:

- neglecting your five-day-a-week exercise program because you do not have enough time

- forgetting to eat correctly and take your vitamins, because it doesn't seem important

- omitting your AA meetings because you don't have time for them

- avoiding your AA sponsor because he just says the same thing every time

- not engaging in activities with your children in the evenings, because you are just too tired

Which healthy coping skills might *you* be tempted to forget about when you're stressed?

_____

_____

_____

_____

4. Behavior changes

You begin acting differently, often after a period of stress. This can take many different forms, including:

- being short-tempered

- becoming very irritable

- blaming others for your mistakes

- being very pessimistic when it comes to problem solving

- denying that you have a problem in the first place

How do *you* act after a stressful period or event?

_____

_____

_____

_____

5. Social isolation and withdrawal

You become isolated, withdrawing from your family or sober friends and returning to your drinking or drugging buddies. Some of the reasons typically given for this withdrawal include:

- "It's too much work to make new friends."

- "People won't like me sober, because I'm boring without a beer."

- "New friends will look down on me because I'm an addict."

- "I don't have anything in common with sober people."

- "Sober people are boring. I need to get out and have some fun and excitement."

What might make *you* want to withdraw from your sober friends, family, or other supportive people?

_____

_____

_____

_____

6. Loss of judgment, loss of control

You make unwise decisions or irrational choices and are not able to stop yourself or undo those choices. This is especially common during the first three to six months of recovery. Warning signs of a lack of judgment or control include:

- going on a spending spree
- yelling at your boss
- bingeing on sweets
- getting in a fight with your spouse
- filing for separation from your spouse

What signs might indicate that *you* have lost your decision-making judgment or are making irrational choices?

_____

_____

_____

_____

7. A change in attitude

You no longer feel that participating in your recovery program is necessary. Or you make a change in your daily routine or life situation that moves you closer to your old drinking or using ways, friends, places, or situations. This may be caused by:

- overconfidence in your newfound sobriety

- a lack of cravings for several days

- the idea that going to AA is too inconvenient

- putting in long hours at work

- focusing on making extra money to pay bills related to your addiction

What might make *you* want to stop participating in your recovery program?

_____

_____

_____

_____

8. Reactivation of denial

You're in denial about your addiction again and probably also denying that you're stressed (*e.g.*, you refuse to talk about your problems or deny their existence). But there may be other reasons why you're back in the denial trap, including:

- you don't believe you did all of those things they say you did when you were addicted

- you blame others or make excuses regarding your past substance use

- you don't believe you need to do everything that your counselor or sponsor insists you should (You think you know more than they do.)

- you refuse to admit or believe that you miss using

- you're afraid to face reality

What is stressing *you* that you might deny or refuse to talk about?

_____

_____

_____

_____

9. Recurrence of physical withdrawal symptoms

You suffer from delayed-onset withdrawal symptoms, which are especially likely to surface when you are stressed. Symptoms may include:

- insomnia

- memory problems

- difficulty in thinking

- lack of concentration or focus

- quick temper

- irritability, lack of patience

- cravings

Which specific delayed withdrawal symptoms might push *you* into a relapse?

_____

_____

_____

_____

These nine warning signs of impending lapse or relapse do not strike in any particular order; they may occur individually or in groups. But the presence of just one of them may be enough to trigger a relapse. It is vital that you become aware of your vulnerable areas and have a plan in place, so you can act as soon as you see *any* sign of trouble.

It is equally important that your family and other members of your support system learn to recognize these signs. Once they know what to look for, they can help you avoid lapsing or relapsing. You will be comforted to know that they can help you, and your family members and friends will undoubtedly be happy to play a part in helping you remain sober.

Preventing Lapse and Relapse

The best way to handle a lapse or relapse is to keep it from happening in the first place! Doing this requires that you master sober life skills, avoid triggers, go to your AA and other meetings regularly, socialize only with sober people, and so on. And you must always have a plan in place for times when you feel yourself slipping.

You've already identified and charted your triggers (Chapter Three), learned the nine warning signs of impending lapse or relapse, and jotted down your own specific warning signs. Now let's zero in on the specific situations that can spell trouble for you and your sobriety.

Rating the Risk of Relapse

It is essential that you think through the situations that are most likely to put you in the danger zone. The Relapse Prediction Scale below lists many situations that might trigger strong urges to drink or use. Look at the items one by one, and imagine yourself in the situation described. Try to feel, hear, and even "taste" yourself in the situation, and decide whether or not the urge to drink or use is there and, if so, whether it is strong or weak. Then rate the strength of the urge and the likelihood of drinking or using on a scale of 0 to 4 (0 is no urge at all, 4 is an irresistible urge). Feel free to add items specific to your situation to the end of the list.

Relapse Prediction Scale

Situations that Might Trigger Strong Urges	Strength of Urge	Likelihood of Using
1. I am in a place where I used alcohol or drugs before.		
2. I am around people I have used alcohol or drugs with before.		
3. I just got paid.		
4. I see coworkers drinking or using.		
5. I am leaving work.		
6. It's Friday night.		
7. I am at a party.		
8. I am thinking of the last time I used.		
9. I feel bored.		
10. I feel great.		
11. I see a lover or ex-lover.		
12. I am having a drink.		
13. My friend is offering me some alcohol or drugs.		
14. I feel sad.		
15. I see a prostitute.		
16. I am out looking for sex.		
17. I feel sexy.		
18. I remember how good a high feels.		
19. I am angry.		
20. I feel stressed out.		
21. I feel guilty.		
22. I just used drugs.		
23. I just broke my abstinence.		
24. I am getting ready for work.		
25. I am tired.		
26. I am frustrated.		

27. I see an anti-drug poster.		
28. I see a pipe.		
29. I am out gambling.		
30. I just had an alcohol or drug dream.		
31. I am watching sports.		
32. I am getting dressed up.		
33. I am under pressure at work.		
34. I am thinking about having sex.		
35. I am angry at my spouse or partner.		
36. My spouse/partner is bugging me about my drinking or using.		
37. My family is bugging me about my drinking or using.		
38. I was just told I have positive urine.		
39. I didn't use, yet my urine was positive.		
40. I am watching an alcohol- or drug-related movie.		
41. I feel anxious.		
42. Someone just criticized me.		
43. I haven't used for a long time.		
44. I feel tense.		
45. Someone I care for is terminally ill.		
46. I am in pain.		
47. I feel burdened.		
48. I am at a bar having a good time.		
49. I had a fight with my family.		
50. I'm tired of my life.		
51.		
52.		
53.		
54.		
55.		

You'll find blank Relapse Prediction Scale forms on www.EnterHealth.com/HealingtheAddictedBrain. Print out several copies, and consider your specific (and probably changing) risks often as you go through recovery.

Resisting the Lapse or Relapse

Now that you know which situations are most likely to trigger a lapse or relapse for you, and the strength of the urge and the likelihood that you will use in a given situation, you can fight back. For some people, handling the signs of impending lapse or relapse will be fairly simple, while for others it may take more planning and effort. Here are four suggestions for building a powerful Lapse/Relapse Prevention Program to safeguard your sobriety. These are certainly not the only approaches, but they've helped many people and can be a good place to start.

1. Lessen your cravings by extinguishing triggers.

Triggers can prompt powerful urges to drink or use, so it's important to learn to extinguish them whenever possible. (See Chapter 3.)

2. Change your social group.

Make it a point to associate exclusively with positive, sober people. Although it sounds easy, this can be a challenge for several reasons. First, you may feel a lot of guilt and shame about your past, so you avoid interacting with healthy people who may not understand you or what you've been through. Second, you may be accustomed to chaotic people and activities. After all that "excitement," interacting with sober people may seem quite dull. Remember, however, that joining the sober crowd can save your marriage, your job, and even your life. And once you develop healthy social skills, you'll find that less chaotic social interactions can be quite pleasant. Finally, there's the fear factor, the feeling that you cannot interact with other people without the "protection" of alcohol or drugs. This issue can, and absolutely should, be dealt with in an intensive outpatient treatment program or individual counseling.

3. Make a schedule for each day.

Plan every day in advance, filling the day with work and activities with positive people you can trust. Don't leave anything to chance, as it's extremely easy to fall back into old, negative habit patterns. Every night, write out a new schedule for the next day, filling up as much time as possible with specific activities. Your schedule may look something like this:

Daily Schedule	
Time	**Activity**
7:00 a.m.	Rise and shine; shower, get dressed; let the dog out, feed the dog
7:30 a.m.	Fix and eat breakfast, leave for work
8:00 a.m.	Work
8:30 a.m.	Work
9:00 a.m.	Work
10:00 a.m.	Work
12:00 noon	Go home; eat lunch, let the dog out, put laundry in washer, go back to work
1:00 p.m.	Work
2:00 p.m.	Work
3:00 p.m.	Work
4:00 p.m.	Work
5:00 p.m.	Leave work; go to gym
6:00 p.m.	Go home; fix dinner, eat, let dog out
6:45 p.m.	Leave for AA meeting
7:00 p.m.	Attend AA meeting

8:00 p.m.	Talk with sponsor
8:30 p.m.	Leave for home
9:00 p.m.	Talk to Mom and Dad, read newspaper, watch TV, check that daily schedule for tomorrow is completed. Note situations that might cause triggers.
11:00 p.m.	Let dog out, brush teeth, go to bed

4. Identify and avoid triggers.

As soon as you finish preparing your daily schedule, update and review your Trigger Inventory, paying close attention to those you are most likely to encounter the next day. (See Chapter Three.) Add the potential triggers you'll likely be facing, as well as how you plan to handle them, to your schedule.

Daily Schedule & Triggers

Time	Activity	Possible Triggers	Plan
7:00 a.m.	Rise and shine; shower, get dressed; let the dog out, feed and water the dog	Have a big presentation at work today	Call co-presenter and review main points before leaving for work
7:30 a.m.	Fix and eat breakfast, leave for work		
8:00 a.m.	Work		
8:30 a.m.	Work	Have to go to Shipping Dept. to get info for report; used to sneak drinks there	Call sponsor before heading into this area, and get a little pep talk

9:00 a.m.	Work	Meeting with sales group; used to drink with them	Use flash cards to review benefits of staying sober
10:00 a.m.	Work		
12:00 noon	Lunch with Jason	He likes to have a beer with lunch	Before going, tell Jason I don't drink anymore and I can't be around it
1:00 p.m.	Work		
2:00 p.m.	Work		
3:00 p.m.	Work	Hungry and tired	Go to snack bar and get a bottle of water and a healthy snack
4:00 p.m.	Work	May be stressed because project is due at 5:00 p.m.	Call Mom for a brief pep talk
5:00 p.m.	Leave work; go to gym to work out.		
6:00 p.m.	Go home; fix dinner, eat, let dog out	Used to drink a lot with dinner	Tell Mom if I am getting cravings
6:45 p.m.	Leave for AA meeting		
7:00 p.m.	Attend AA meeting	May hear too many "use and abuse stories"	Zero in on the healthy coping behaviors that others have used

8:00 p.m.	Talk with sponsor		
8:30 p.m.	Leave for home		
9:00 p.m.	Talk to Mom and Dad, read newspaper, watch TV, fill out daily schedule for tomorrow, note situations that might cause triggers.	May get bored	TiVo some good shows so I have plenty to watch
11:00 p.m.	Let dog out, brush teeth, go to bed		

The Emergency Lapse/Relapse Prevention Plan

A simple yet effective method is to create an Emergency Lapse/Relapse Prevention Plan, a set of responses to the urge to drink or use. Using your answers to the Relapse Prediction Scale, list the situations that you believe present the greatest danger of lapse or relapse. Then list the steps you can take to handle these situations without using alcohol or drugs. As an example, check out the plan that follows, created by my patient Heather.

Heather's Emergency Lapse/Relapse Prevention Plan

Relapse Danger #1: Missing going to parties and getting drunk and high, feeling bored

Steps I can take to handle this situation without using alcohol or drugs:

1. Keep involved in meetings and activities so I can find other sober or clean people to learn what they are doing to cope with boredom.

2. Call my sponsor or other sober friends when my boredom gets me thinking about getting drunk or high. Ask them to get together to hang or do something like go to a movie or go to the Y to shoot hoops.

3. Make a detailed plan for every weekend, because this is the time I feel most bored.

4. Take up a new hobby that will help keep me busy and make me feel good. My son is into collecting rocks. I'm going to take him to the library so we can get books about rock collecting.

Relapse Danger #2: Feeling depressed about my life and how I messed it up

Steps I can take to handle this situation without using alcohol or drugs:

1. Keep reminding myself that it will take time to get my life together now that I've quit alcohol and drugs.

2. Focus on the positive things I have—my son and daughter, my husband, my good friends, my job, my improved health.

3. Keep up my recovery disciplines, especially when I don't feel like it and want to blow off meetings.

4. Talk about how I feel, and get support from those in the program.

Here's a blank form you can use to create your own prevention plan. Make several copies of the blank form so you can continually update your plan.

My Emergency Lapse/Relapse Prevention Plan

Relapse Danger #1: _____

Steps I can take to handle this situation without using alcohol or drugs:

1. _____

2. _____

3. _____

4. _____

Relapse Danger #2: _____

Steps I can take to handle this situation without using alcohol or drugs:

1. _____

2. _____

3. _____

4. _____

Relapse Danger #3: _____

Steps I can take to handle this situation without using alcohol or drugs:

1. _____

2. _____

3. _____

4. _____

What to Do If You Slip

If you do experience a lapse or relapse, try to do everything you can to "shut it down" immediately. Of course, this can be difficult to do on your own when you're drinking or using and the logic centers of your brain are no longer in command. That's where the Lapse/Relapse Action Plan (see below) can be a lifesaver. The Lapse/Relapse Action Plan is a list of things that you can do immediately to stop a lapse or relapse in its tracks. Make several copies of the form below, and fill in the names and phone numbers of those who are in a position to help you. Then put copies in your wallet or purse, car, desk, locker, or anywhere else where you can lay your hands on it in an emergency.

LAPSE/RELAPSE ACTION PLAN

WHO TO CALL	NAME, PHONE NUMBER
	List the names and phone numbers of five people who will support you in your sobriety.
	1. _____
	2. _____
	3. _____
	4. _____
	5. _____
	Call one of the names on this list immediately, and keep calling until you find someone who can talk to you and help you hang on to your sober lifestyle.

WHAT TO DO	1. *Take immediate action:* Get up and leave the area. If you are in your own house, get out and go to a neutral area where you will be in the company of those who will support your sobriety.
	2. *Keep it in perspective:* Remind yourself that having one slip does not have to lead to a full-blown relapse. Tell yourself, "I will *not* give in to feelings of guilt or blame, because I know these feelings will pass in time."
	3. *Take follow-up action:* Examine the lapse at the next session with your therapist, discuss the events prior to the lapse, and identify the triggers and your reactions to them. Work with your therapist to set up a plan for coping with similar situations in the future.
REMEMBER: This is only a temporary detour on the road to sobriety!	

Issues to Explore in the Aftermath of a Lapse or Relapse

Even if you do everything suggested in this chapter, you may still lapse or relapse occasionally. Rather than kicking yourself for "failing," focus on the future. Once you have returned to sobriety, learn from the experience. Turn a negative into a positive by using this lapse or relapse as an opportunity to learn how to avoid another one.

Working with your therapist, counselor, or sponsor, examine what happened, then adjust your program. For example, you might discuss the following:

• Are you taking the right medicines? The right dosages?

• Are you going to 12-step groups often enough? To the right groups?

• Are you going to outpatient treatment often enough?

- Are you seeing your therapist often enough?

- Are you contacting your sponsor often enough?

- Are certain activities your triggers? Should you look for different activities?

- Are certain friends your triggers? Do you need to avoid them? To look for new, sober friends?

You may find it necessary to fine-tune your anti-addiction medication, add or adjust a psychiatric medication for any co-occurring psychiatric disorders, increase the frequency of your 12-step group attendance, talk to your sponsor more often, or increase the number of meetings you have with your individual alcohol or drug counselor.

Slow down, follow through, and learn: these are the best responses to a lapse or relapse.

And when you look back on the lapse or relapse, remind yourself that you are *not* a failure. There was a problem with one or more of the components of your recovery program, a problem that can be fixed. Like the diabetic who used the improper dose of insulin and suffered the health consequences, you miscalculated. Now is the time to reexamine and retool your recovery program to prevent further lapses and relapses.

Danny, a thirty-five-year-old freelance construction worker, had an on-again, off-again relationship with alcohol. He began drinking when he was fifteen years old, and by the time he was twenty, he was drinking on a nightly basis to the point of passing out. Danny's parents put him in a month-long rehab program when he was sixteen, and he got sober for about six months. But then he got involved with a rough crowd and started drinking again. Over the next eighteen years, Danny bounced in and out of rehab five times. Each time, he went back to drinking almost as soon as he got out. Finally, when Danny had lost his family, his career, and just about every ounce of his self-respect, he committed himself 100 percent to getting sober. He sat down and made a list of everything he could think of that seemed to trigger his drinking. Then, with the help of a psychotherapist who specialized in addiction, Danny came up with a number of ways to either avoid those triggers or handle them in healthier ways. The first (and perhaps most important) thing that he did was to stop hanging out with his old drinking buddies. Danny began taking Vivitrol, attending daily AA meetings, and working with his therapist on the inaccurate thoughts that kept his alcoholism in play. He made up a daily schedule that included a plan for handling triggers and devised an Emergency Relapse Response Plan for those times when he felt a strong urge to drink. It's been eighteen months since Danny began this new phase of life, and he has remained alcohol-free the entire time, the longest period of sobriety he's ever experienced.

You Don't Have to Be a Victim!

Many addicts in recovery think that lapses and relapses "just happen" and that there's nothing they can do about them other than hope they don't destroy the recovery process.

But now *you* know that relapse is a normal part of the chronic disease called addiction, with clearly identifiable signs of impending trouble. This means that you (and your support system) can watch for these signs and get help before the lapse or relapse is under way. And if you do slip, you can get back on track quickly. By using the techniques discussed in this chapter, you *can* regain control and salvage your sobriety, even when the urge to drink or use seems insurmountable.

Key Points Review

- A lapse is a slip, a "whoops" moment. A relapse is a substantial period of alcohol or drug use during which you go back to the levels of usage and behaviors seen in your active addiction.

- The events leading to a relapse can be so subtle and so easily explained away that the relapse itself can feel like it happened suddenly.

- However, the truth is that lapse or relapse does *not* just happen. It's the result of a process that can take up to several weeks to develop.

- You can and must learn to recognize the signs of impending relapse, which begin with negative changes in attitudes, feelings, and behaviors.

- People, places, situations, or events that remind you of times when you were drinking or using drugs (triggers) can be dangerous to your sobriety.

- You can help prevent relapse by identifying and avoiding your triggers, extinguishing your triggers, changing your social group, making a schedule for each and every day, and creating an Emergency Lapse/Relapse Prevention Plan.

- If you do experience a lapse, slow down and focus. Then follow through with your Lapse/Relapse Action Plan. Keep reminding yourself that you *can* get back on track, and you *can* learn a great deal from the experience so that particular mistake will not happen again.

CHAPTER TEN

Health and Nutrition in Recovery

Addiction is the nation's top health problem, causing more illnesses, disabilities, and deaths than any other preventable health problem. Addiction destroys the health of people of all ages, both genders, and every ethnic group, and its devastating physical impact involves nearly every part of the body. Heavy drinking is linked to brain damage, anemia, liver disease, nerve problems, bleeding ulcers, increased infections, elevated blood pressure, and a higher risk of developing certain forms of cancer. Drug abuse is associated with bronchitis, heart damage, blindness, seizures, perforation of the nasal bone, blood clots, kidney failure, TB, hepatitis, and an increased susceptibility to infections including HIV/AIDS. Some of these problems may surface only after prolonged use or the ingestion of high doses of the drug, but others can occur in response to a single episode.

These health problems are not only of concern when your addiction is active. Even after you get sober—perhaps long after—you may continue to suffer the health consequences of your addiction and be forced to pay strict attention to your physical health.

In this chapter, I'll explain how alcohol and drugs can attack physical health. Then I'll lay out the elements of a healthy diet and an effective exercise plan, along with tips and worksheets that can help you stay on course.

Health Risks Associated with Alcohol and Drug Use

Alcoholism and heavy drinking can cause health and functional problems that affect the body from head to toe. The effects of chronic excessive alcohol ingestion on various parts of the body and body systems include decreased ability to learn and remember, impaired judgment, loss of ability to reason, poor memory and concentration, premature aging of the brain, heart attack, heart failure, high blood pressure, irregular heartbeat, stroke, night blindness, life-threatening bleeding from the esophagus and stomach, stomach or intestinal ulcers, cirrhosis of the liver, fatty liver resulting in poor liver function, hepatitis, respiratory depression leading to death, disruption of sexual hormones, fetal abnormalities, fetal alcohol syndrome, anemia (low blood count), increased infections due to impaired immunity, nerve damage, osteoporosis, pancreatitis, and cancer of the breast, esophagus, stomach, rectum, liver, mouth, and throat. In addition, heavy alcohol use and alcoholism increase the chances of dying due to drowning, homicide, suicide, motor vehicle crashes, and sexually transmitted diseases (including HIV infection).

The physical effects of drug abuse can include brain damage, chromosome damage, chronic bronchitis, increased susceptibility to infections, loss of energy, abdominal cramps and diarrhea, chronic constipation, slow and confused thinking, blindness, delirium, hallucinations or paranoia, heart attack, kidney failure, perforated nasal septum (the bone and cartilage that divides the nasal cavity in two), seizures, stroke, blood clots to the heart, lung, or brain, reduction of male and female sex hormones, slowing the breathing to the point of coma or death, and lung cancer.

If you suffer from any medical issues related to your addiction, see your physician and get them treated!

How Alcohol and Drugs Interfere with Good Nutrition

When you're in the throes of an addiction, you are likely to eat erratically, skip meals, eat mostly unhealthy food, or overeat. If you have an alcohol problem, for example, at the peak of your drinking you may have been ingesting as much as 50 percent of your total daily calories from alcohol. If you've been addicted to drugs, you may very well have spent your food budget on your substance of choice rather than nutrient-rich foods. Stimulants may have interfered with your ability to take in sufficient nutrients by suppressing your appetite. Or repeated marijuana highs may have spurred you to consume huge amounts of candy, potato chips, cake, and cookies.

As a result of chronic poor nutrition, your hunger and satiety signals may have become weakened, confused, or may even be completely absent. Your metabolic rate may be sky-high or very low. You may be overweight or underweight, bloated, fatigued, depressed, irritable, or anxious. And your body may have a difficult time healing itself, because it doesn't have the proper tools. Dehydration is also common during the withdrawal stabilization phase.

Now that you are sober and your body is trying to normalize, it is wise to provide it with a highly nutritious diet, giving it the tools it needs to repair the various injured systems and parts. But before we delve into the elements of a nutritious diet, let's first take a look at how addictive substances affect your nutritional status.

Alcohol

Alcoholism impairs two major organs involved in metabolism and nutrition: the liver and the pancreas. The liver helps filter waste and harmful substances from the blood, breaking down these poisons before they can get to other parts of the body. Unfortunately, the poisons also kill many liver cells and, over time, impair its function. The pancreas regulates blood sugar and fat absorption. Hindering or harming either of these organs results in an imbalance of fluids, calories, electrolytes, and vitamins. Both are also highly susceptible to developing cancer due to alcohol toxicity.

Even if it doesn't destroy the liver or pancreas, alcohol depletes the body of B vitamins, vitamin A, and vitamin C, all of which are essential for healthy physiological functioning. In order to metabolize alcohol, the body needs greater than normal amounts of certain B vitamins (thiamine, riboflavin, B$_6$, and folic acid). There is also an increased need for B vitamins to rebuild the bodily systems damaged by chronic alcohol ingestion. Unfortunately, even as alcohol "chews up" B vitamins, it interferes with the body's ability to absorb these nutrients. Making matters worse, drinkers often substitute alcohol for food, so their intake of B vitamins is low to begin with.

The insufficient intake and difficulty absorbing and storing the B vitamins, coupled with the body's increased need for them, can trigger serious problems including anemia, muscle and nervous tissue damage, as well as neurological problems such as Korsakoff's syndrome, which causes short-term memory loss and difficulty learning new information.

In addition, alcohol-related deficiencies of vitamin A can cause night blindness and impaired vision, while too little vitamin C can weaken the immune system, among other things. Other nutritional complications of alcoholism include permanent liver damage (or cirrhosis), seizures, diabetes, severe malnutrition, and osteoporosis in postmenopausal women.

Opiates

Opiates, including heroin and prescription narcotics such as codeine and morphine, cause the gastrointestinal system to slow down markedly. This explains why constipation is a very common symptom of opiate addiction.

Stimulants

Using stimulants such as crack, cocaine, and methamphetamine significantly decreases the appetite, resulting in weight loss and eventual malnutrition. Elevated blood pressure, increased heart rate, insomnia, dehydration, and electrolyte imbalances can all occur as a result of stimulant abuse, especially over time. Stimulants rev up the metabolism by increasing production of adrenaline, which in turn uses up protein in the body and destroys lean body mass. Once stimulant use ceases, the appetite can return with a vengeance, causing unwanted weight gain.

Marijuana

Marijuana can increase the appetite, especially for carbohydrates, so some long-term users may become overweight.

These are just some of the nutritional deficits associated with alcohol and drug abuse, and they are all potentially serious. Another concern is the fact that addicts often confuse hunger and thirst signals with drug cravings, which means that simply getting hungry or thirsty may trigger a lapse or relapse. That's why it's imperative that your recovery program includes a dietary component so you can relearn how to eat properly and replenish your body's store of nutrients.

 You'll find a great deal of helpful information on addiction and nutrition—over four hours' worth—that will help you customize your diet to your lifestyle and tastes. You'll also learn about the value of vitamins and minerals, and how to incorporate optimal amounts of these nutrients into your diet. See the nutrition e-sessions on www.EnterHealth.com/ HealingtheAddictedBrain.

Elements of a Healthful Diet

A healthful, balanced diet provides your body with the nutritional tools it needs to heal quickly and effectively. Eating regularly, drinking sufficient amounts of fluids, and consuming a highly nutritious diet can help to:

- furnish sufficient energy for recovery
- decrease alcohol and drug cravings
- improve sleep quality and duration
- increase mental concentration
- decrease withdrawal-related anxiety and depression
- stabilize weight
- normalize hunger and satiety signals

But what is a healthful, balanced diet? Many who have been caught in the web of addiction have had erratic eating habits for years or even decades and no longer know. Using the U.S. government's Food Guide Pyramid as the basis of a good diet, I'll help you figure out what, when, and how to eat—all of which are important elements in your recovery and the reestablishment of your good health.

Although it may not be exciting, the Food Guide Pyramid is the most solid, reliable guide to healthy eating that I've ever seen. It's not a diet; it's an eating plan that tells you the kinds and amounts of foods you should be consuming daily as a minimum. You can eat more servings of these foods if you want, but not less. Remember that skipping meals or eating less than the minimum will compromise your nutritional status and may make you more likely to relapse.

With that in mind, take a look at the kinds and amounts of foods your body needs on a daily basis.

What to Eat

The basic idea behind the Food Pyramid is to consume the bulk of your daily foods from the grain group, have plenty of fruits and vegetables, eat small amounts of lean protein, and include a few servings of dairy. Add fats, oils, and sweets sparingly, primarily to flavor your foods. Choose the foods that you really like from each group, and vary your choices. The result should be meals that are tasty, appealing, and very nutritious.

Grains

Daily servings: 6–11

Serving size: ½ cup cooked cereal, pasta, or rice; one slice of bread; 1 oz. cereal

What grains do for you: Grains contain complex carbohydrates, which are broken down into glucose, the body's fuel. Complex carbohydrates help stabilize the blood sugar and increase the production of serotonin, a neurotransmitter that plays an important part in warding off depression and increasing the feeling of well-being. Grains also provide B vitamins, which are notoriously deficient in alcoholics.

Fruits and Vegetables

Daily servings: 2–4 servings fruits, plus 3–5 servings vegetables

Serving size: 1 cup chopped raw fruits or vegetables; 1 medium-sized fruit; ½ cup fruit or vegetable juice

What fruits and vegetables do for you: Fruits and vegetables provide vitamin C, beta-carotene, fiber, folate, and phytochemicals that help the body fight disease. Addicts are often deficient in vitamin C, folate, and beta-carotene (vitamin A) and have compromised immune systems, so this food group can be particularly helpful. Fruits and vegetables also contain fiber, which can ease constipation. Try to eat your fruits and vegetables as close to raw as possible and limit fruit or vegetable juice to one serving per day.

Protein

Daily servings: 2–3

Serving size: 2–3 oz. cooked meat, fish, or poultry; 2 eggs; 1 cup cooked dry beans, peas, or lentils; ½ cup nuts; 4 tablespoons of peanut butter

What protein does for you: Protein is used to build and maintain tissues, manufacture hormones and enzymes, maintain fluid balance, and create antibodies to fight disease. It also helps to stabilize blood sugar levels. Beans, peas, and lentils are particularly good protein choices because they're high in vitamins and fiber, yet low in fat. Include them in your diet often.

Dairy Foods

Daily servings: 2–3

Serving size: 1 cup milk or yogurt; 1½–2 oz. cheese

What dairy foods do for you: Dairy foods are an excellent source of calcium, protein, and vitamin D, all of which contribute to the growth and maintenance of bones and teeth. Too little calcium can result in osteoporosis, the thinning of the bones that can lead to fractures and deformities of the spine.

Fats, Oils, and Sweets

Daily servings: At least one serving per day, but use sparingly

Serving size: 1 tablespoon oil, butter, mayonnaise

What fats, oils, and sweets do for you: Getting a little fat or oil into the diet is necessary to meet your requirement for essential fatty acids, which play a part in the formation of cell membranes, production of hormone-like compounds, immunity, and vision. Fats and sweets add palatability to foods and enjoyment to meals. The trick is to keep from overdoing either one.

Meal Planning

Addicts have learned to act on impulse, and this is almost always reflected in their eating habits. Irregular meals, eating on the run, and choosing foods for their taste rather than their nutritional value isn't the exception: it's the rule! More often than not, there is no set schedule for meals, an absence of meal planning, and an overreliance on high-calorie, high-fat fast foods such as hamburgers, fried foods, and sweets. However, with a little planning, eating can be transformed from an impulsive activity to an important and healthy component of recovery.

A healthful, balanced meal or snack should contain a grain, a fruit or vegetable, and some protein or dairy (since dairy also contains protein). The grains, fruits, and vegetables provide energy, while the protein and dairy help keep blood sugar stable.

Take a look at the following meal and snack plan, which is based on the minimum daily number of servings from each food group. Remember that you can add more servings according to your size, energy needs, and your gender (men need more calories). But don't take away any servings, or you'll be cheating your body out of much-needed nutrients.

Sample Meal and Snack Plan

Breakfast

   1 serving grains (*e.g.*, 1 oz. whole-grain cereal)

   ½ serving protein (*e.g.*, 1 egg)

   ½ serving dairy (*e.g.*, ½ cup nonfat milk)

   1 serving fruit (*e.g.*, 1 orange)

Lunch

   2 servings grains (*e.g.*, 2 pieces whole grain bread)

   1 serving protein (*e.g.*, 3 oz. tuna fish)

   1 serving vegetables (*e.g.*, 1 sliced tomato)

   1 serving fat (*e.g.*, 1 tablespoon mayonnaise)

Snack

   1 serving grains (*e.g.*, 1 bran muffin)

   ½ serving dairy (*e.g.*, 1 oz. cheese)

   1 serving vegetables (*e.g.*, 1 cup carrot sticks)

Dinner

   2 serving grains (*e.g.*, ½ cup rice; 1 roll)

   1 serving protein (*e.g.*, 3 oz. broiled salmon)

   1 serving vegetables (*e.g.*, ½ cup cooked green beans)

Snack

   1 serving grains (*e.g.*, 1 piece cinnamon toast)

   1 serving dairy (*e.g.*, 1 cup yogurt)

   1 serving fruit (*e.g.*, 1 cup strawberries)

Depending upon your prior lifestyle and substance of abuse, this may seem like either an awful lot of food or too little. Keep in mind that this meal plan is a place to start, a way to get back in touch with what you should be eating on a daily basis. Remember that you can eat more servings—this *isn't* about starving yourself!—but not fewer servings. You need this much healthful food to ensure you're getting adequate amounts of all the nutrients. Eventually your body will become more acclimated to proper eating, and you may be able to depend more heavily on your body's natural hunger and satiety signals. For now, however, you'll need to encourage yourself to eat on a schedule and include planned foods in planned amounts. For help in implementing this plan and for answers to any questions, consult a nutritionist or your healthcare provider.

Suggestions for Meal Planning

- *Plan a week's meals*—It's practically impossible to eat a well-balanced diet without figuring out just what you're going to eat and when you're going to eat it. Eating on the run or grabbing whatever happens to be in the refrigerator is guaranteed to result in poor eating habits. Take the time once a week to plan a week's meals, make a grocery list, and do the shopping all at once. It may feel like a big chore but will actually save you time and lower your stress levels during the week. It will also save you a significant amount of money.

- *Include exceptions*—Most people enjoy eating out from time to time, going to a friend's house for dinner, or going to parties. Plan these events in advance, and figure them into the schedule rather than deciding to eat out on the spur of the moment, which can lead to impulsive (and unhealthy) eating behaviors.

- *Start your day with breakfast*—Breakfast fills your "empty tank" to get you going after several hours without food. Skipping breakfast slows your metabolism and makes you more prone to bingeing on high-calorie, low-nutrient foods.

- *Snack smart*—Snacks are a great way to refuel and to add nutritious foods to your diet. Healthy snacks can also taste great—try an apple or celery sticks with peanut butter, low-fat cheese with whole-grain crackers, raisins, whole-grain toast with low-sugar jam, or a bowl of whole-grain cereal. Bananas, strawberries, and melons are great-tasting fruits. You can satisfy your taste buds and improve your health at the same time.

Exercise, the World's Best Stress Reliever

Most people turn to alcohol or drugs as a way to escape stress. But this "solution" backfires by creating endless problems and multiplying stress a thousandfold. A much more efficient way to handle stress is adding exercise to the other stress-reduction techniques discussed in Chapter Three. Aerobic exercise, which includes activities like running, brisk walking, playing tennis, dancing continuously, or cycling, is extremely effective as an anxiety buster and mood elevator. It burns stress hormones as well as calories, relieves muscle tension, and promotes the release of the body's feel-good hormones, the endorphins. It also improves the ability to concentrate and think clearly.

Aerobic exercise is even more beneficial when it's part of a larger five-part exercise program:

- *Warm-up*—Increase your muscle temperature and get your blood moving by doing five to ten minutes of jogging in place, fast walking, jumping rope, or using the stair climber at an easy pace. An easy but thorough warm-up will help prevent injuries and prime your body for more intense exercise.

- *Aerobic exercise*—Once you start to feel warm, you can increase the intensity with aerobic exercises, the kind that make your heart beat faster and your breathing deeper. Examples including jogging, cycling, swimming, fast walking, and climbing stairs. If you haven't exercised in a while, limit the aerobic portion of your plan to five to ten minutes at the beginning. Then, as you grow stronger, increase the time in small increments until you're doing twenty to thirty minutes at a time, at least every other day.

- *Strengthening exercises*—Strengthening occurs as a result of pitting your muscles against another force (whether it's weights, gravity, water, or each other) and gradually increasing the length of time that you do so. Examples of strengthening exercises include weightlifting, pushups, leg lifts, isometric exercises, and swimming. Begin with ten to fifteen minutes every other day, and gradually work your way up to twenty to thirty minutes. (Do your strengthening exercises on the days that you don't do your aerobic exercises.)

- *Stretching*—A great way to relieve muscle tension and ease stress, stretching increases the range of motion in your joints and increases the elasticity of your muscles. (It's a good idea to consult a physical trainer or a stretch expert when you're first learning to stretch, to make sure you do it properly. Stretching the wrong way can cause injury.) Always stretch slowly and carefully; be sure your body is thoroughly warmed up before stretching, and relax into the stretch at your maximum position for at least thirty seconds to allow the muscles to respond. Stretching should be done after both aerobic and strengthening exercises. A daily stretching session lasting ten to fifteen minutes is a good antidote to anxiety.

- *Cool-down*—The opposite of the warm-up, the cool-down is designed to reduce your heart rate and body temperature and bring your body back to normal after an exercise session. Slow walking and stretching are two great ways to cool down.

Be sure to check with your physician before starting any new physical exercise plan!

Sample Exercise Plan

Following is a plan that includes the various kinds and amounts of recommended types of exercises, spread out over a seven-day period. Just insert your favorite kinds of aerobic, strengthening, and stretching exercises into the template, start with the shorter sessions, and gradually increase your time. As you become stronger, you will also want to gradually increase the amount of force your muscles exert (*e.g.*, increase the amount of weight you're lifting). Now you've got a custom-made plan!

Exercise Plan

<u>Monday</u>

Warm-up (5–10 minutes)

Aerobic exercises (5–30 minutes)

Cool-down (5–10 minutes)

<u>Tuesday</u>

Warm-up (5–10 minutes)

Strengthening exercises (10–30 minutes)

Stretching (10–15 minutes)

Cool-down (5–10 minutes)

<u>Wednesday</u>

Warm-up (5–10 minutes)

Aerobic exercises (5–30 minutes)

Cool-down (5–10 minutes)

<u>Thursday</u>

Warm-up (5–10 minutes)

Strengthening exercises (10–30 minutes)

Stretching (10–15 minutes)

Cool-down (5–10 minutes)

Friday

Warm-up (5–10 minutes)

Aerobic exercises (5–30 minutes)

Cool-down (5–10 minutes)

Saturday

Warm-up (5–10 minutes)

Strengthening exercises (10–30 minutes)

Stretching (10–15 minutes)

Cool-down (5–10 minutes)

Sunday

Day off

Tips for Getting More Exercise in Your Life

Not all of your exercising has to take place at a gym. Opportunities to exercise abound in your everyday life. You just have to become aware of them.

- Walk, bike, or jog to see friends.
- Take a ten-minute activity break every hour when reading or watching TV.
- Climb the stairs instead of taking an escalator or elevator.
- Get an exercise partner (being active is much more fun with friends or family).
- Park farther away and walk.
- Plan and take part in one special physical activity each week, like a bike ride or a group hike.

- Join in physical activities at school or at work (intramural sports, softball team at work, the gym at your workplace, swimming class at your local college).

- Be adventurous: try waterskiing, ballroom dancing, or tae kwan do.

Some people need to set aside specific times for exercise in the weekly schedule. If you're one of these people, make an appointment with yourself to do something active! In fact, it is helpful to put the exercise plan (pages 249–50) into your weekly schedule. It may also be helpful to hire a personal trainer to help you customize and get started on your exercise program, someone you can check in with from time to time to make any necessary adjustments to your program and to help keep you on track.

You Can Do It!

It may have been years since you ate well and exercised; the whole idea of sitting down to regular meals and exercising every day may seem strange and awkward. Don't worry if you're not eating and exercising to perfection on day one. Just as with every part of recovery, it takes a while to learn to do this well, to make it a lifelong habit. Take it one meal, one exercise session at a time, and over time you'll find it becoming easier and easier. And you'll find your health becoming stronger and stronger while your cravings and desire to use become weaker and weaker.

Key Points Review

- The substances and behaviors associated with addiction can be very damaging to your physical health.

- Heavy drinking can trigger physical damage to the brain, liver, nerves, immune system, and other parts of the body.

- Drug abuse can damage the heart, eyes, kidneys, and other organs, and increase the risk of suffering from blood clots, HIV/AIDS, TB, hepatitis, and other serious diseases.

- Addicts often eat poorly and focus on foods with little nutritional value, leading to nutritional deficits that can harm the body.

- Alcohol depletes the body of the B family of vitamins, among other nutrients.

- Opiates can interfere with the healthy functioning of the gastrointestinal system.

- Stimulants can raise the blood pressure and heart rate and trigger dehydration and electrolyte imbalances.

- Marijuana can increase the appetite, especially the hunger for non-nutritious foods.

- A health-enhancing diet provides ample energy and nutrients for body repair and helps speed the recovery process.

- The U.S. government's Food Guide Pyramid is a reliable guide to healthy eating.

- Exercise helps reduce stress and relieve depression, thereby lessening the chance of lapse or relapse.

- A well-rounded exercise program should include aerobic, strengthening, and stretching exercises.

- Your diet and exercise regimen does not have to be overly difficult or absolutely perfect. With simple changes and a little planning, you can improve your physical health, reduce the risk of relapse, and help heal the brain damage caused by addiction.

CHAPTER ELEVEN

Regaining Enjoyment and Pleasure

The desire for happiness is universal, and we've found many ways to make ourselves happy. Sometimes, we forget what real happiness is, or we don't know how to achieve it. Instead, we settle for simply holding off unhappy feelings. As one patient said, "You know, doc, it used to seem like I was happy when I was drinking. I went out with friends all the time, and we drank until we were blotto, barfing, and broke. Wow, can you believe I thought that was happiness?"

I *can* believe she thought that was happiness, because many people with addictions don't know what happiness is. However, they certainly know what sadness is. Depression, stress, anxiety, and numerous other negative feelings are well known to most addicts. In fact, the purpose of drinking or using is to ward off such feelings and somehow "get happy." But addicts often have no idea what true happiness is. And once alcohol and drugs are no longer "managing" their feelings and fooling them into thinking they're happy, they simply don't know what to do with themselves.

Believe it or not, happiness is the result of a conscious choice to think the thoughts that lead to the beliefs and behaviors that can bring you joy. Happiness is everywhere. It can be found in helping others, succeeding at a task, loving and being loved, or appreciating beauty. It can be found in jokes, movies, books, conversation, warm friendships, athletic activity, singing, dancing, or helping a toddler learn a new word.

Happiness—sober happiness—plays an extremely important role in successful recovery and is well within your reach. In this chapter, I explore the many roads that can lead to happiness.

The Importance of Happiness in Sobriety

Jacob, a sixty-eight-year-old retired teacher, came to me at the request of his wife for help with his alcohol problem. In the initial interview, he told me that he knew that he drank a lot, but he really didn't think it was a problem. "Look, doc," he said. "I worked my whole life until just last year. Now I'm retired. Why can't I have a few drinks and enjoy myself?" When I pointed out that his wife said his alcoholism was endangering his health, their marriage, and his relationships with others, he replied, "The thing is, I just can't imagine living without having a drink now and then. Truly, I'm happiest when I've had a few. And if I thought I'd never be able to have another beer or glass of scotch, I just don't know if I'd want to go on living."

It *can* be hard to relax and enjoy life while in recovery. First, there are the confusing and stressful changes in thinking necessary for a successful recovery. Then there's the nonnegotiable fact that you can't turn to alcohol or drugs when you want to feel better or have fun. Neither can you hang around with your old drinking or using buddies or go to many of the places you used to enjoy, because they are triggers for your addictive behaviors. Then there are the physical changes in your brain, such as those excess "give me a beer" receptors screaming to be satisfied. Topping it all off, you may be wrestling with major difficulties as you struggle to reestablish trust within your family, repair damaged relationships, rebuild your finances, and so on. And you may feel extremely guilty about various things you did while drinking or using.

The new pressures of living as a sober person can mount quickly, while the new pleasures may come much more slowly. Learning to enjoy life again can be a trial-and-error process that takes time, and we don't always know where to begin. What we do know is that socializing and being involved in various activities can produce a great deal of pleasure. Conversely, the active addiction process is very isolating, as addicts usually spend a great deal of their day, if not their entire day, alone or only with other users. One of your tasks in recovery will be to figure out which activities give you pleasure and can be enjoyed with clean and sober family members, friends, and acquaintances.

You might not realize it, but most pleasures are learned. Whatever your favorite activity, recreation, or sport, there's a good chance you had to learn to enjoy it. You've probably forgotten how much time and effort you had to put in to master baseball, soccer, or bridge, understand photography, learn the techniques of fishing, acquire an appreciation of art or music, reach level ten on the latest computer game, master conversation skills, and so on.

Remember how decidedly "un-fun" it was as you struggled to learn the rules, techniques, or skills of your favorite activity? (How many thousands of tennis balls did you hit against a wall before you could play a decent game of tennis? How many times did you have to untangle the fishing line before you mastered casting? How many times did you fall off of your bike before you finally learned to ride it?) Eventually, participating in and excelling at your favorite activity became second nature, and you were able to enjoy yourself. Learning to have "sober" fun will most likely be a similar experience.

Recovering addicts have often had limited experience as adults with alcohol-free or drug-free recreation and social activities. They may have been caught up in addiction for so long that they've forgotten how to have fun that isn't related to substance abuse. They may not even remember which non-alcohol or non-drug activities brought them pleasure or helped them relax. And even if they do remember, they may have lost the skills necessary to enjoy those activities—skills as simple as baking cookies or as complex as building a model ship in a bottle. And they may have no idea how to gain (or regain) such skills. The answer is simple: jump in with both feet.

Reclaiming Happiness

Happiness is a natural goal for children, but in adulthood this goal can mutate into a striving for material goods. However, materialism rarely satisfies for long. You might think that acquiring that home, boat, or fancy television is the recipe for happiness, but the excitement only lasts for a short while. In no time at all, you'll need some new purchase to rev up those happy, excited feelings. The same is true of drinking and using drugs. You may think that getting high will make you happy or take away the bad feelings. But all too soon the good feelings fade, leaving emptiness and countless problems that require another high to assuage them.

To get back on the road to happiness, you'll first need to acknowledge that your current strategies for finding happiness aren't working and that it's time to make smarter choices. One of the first choices should be to change your thoughts, which can have a major impact on your ability to find happiness. Begin with the belief that you deserve happiness and have the power to change your life. You must also get involved in new kinds of activities and spend time with new and sober people.

There are endless ways of having fun and finding happiness that don't involve alcohol or drugs. Take a look at the following lists of relaxing and fun things that you may want to try. Circle those that you enjoyed in the past or think you might enjoy in the future:

Activities		
Recreational Activities (performed in a sober environment)		
Acting class	Antiquing	Archery
Attending a concert	Attending an auction	Attending interesting lectures

Basketball at the park	Bicycling around the neighborhood	Birdwatching
Boating	Bowling	Building an aquarium
Camping or back-packing trip	Canoeing	Card games
Chess or checkers	Collecting coins	Cooking, or learning to cook
Dancing	Decorating a room	Designing and cultivating a garden in your backyard
Exercising	Fishing	Flying a kite
Getting involved in local politics	Going to a baseball, football, or soccer game with (sober) friends	Going for a drive
Going out for dinner (without having alcoholic drinks)	Going to art exhibits	Going to museums
Going to the beach	Going to the movies or the theater	Going to the opera
Going to the zoo	Golfing	Hiking
Horseback riding	Ice skating	Jogging
Learning to knit	Learning to macramé	Learning to box
Learning to paint	Learning to sculpt	Learning to throw pottery
Learning woodworking	Lifting weights at the gym	Listening to relaxing music
Making model airplanes, cars, or ships	Needlepoint	Picnicking with a friend or family member
Playing ping pong	Playing a musical instrument	Playing board games

Playing card games	Playing chess	Playing Frisbee
Playing racquetball	Playing tennis	Playing touch football
Playing video games	Reading	Reading joke books or finding jokes online
Rock climbing	Rollerblading	Sailing or boating
Scuba diving	Shooting pool	Shopping at flea markets
Shuffleboard	Sightseeing	Singing (by yourself or in a group)
Skiing	Skydiving	Stamp collecting
Studying photography	Sunbathing	Surfboarding
Surfing	Swimming	Taking a flower arranging class
Taking a walk in a nearby park	Taking art classes	Taking long walks
Talking with friends	Volunteering	Working on crossword puzzles
Working on a car	Writing in a journal	
Fun Sports/Exercises		
Ballet	Ballroom dancing	Baseball
Basketball	Belly dancing	Country dancing
Folk dancing	Hockey	Jazzercise
Latin dancing	Martial arts	Modern dancing
Softball	T'ai chi	Tap dancing
Touch football	Water aerobics	

Hopefully, you circled lots of activities in the lists above.

Next, list every activity or hobby you circled on a separate piece of paper. Put them in order, beginning with those you think might be the most fun. Now, pick one or two from the upper part of the list, and do them. Don't worry about looking silly, and don't try to be perfect. Just do them! (Be sure to check with your physician before beginning a new form of exercise.)

Interacting with Sober Friends and Groups

Solitary pleasures such as reading, working on crossword puzzles, watching television, and walking or shopping alone can be relaxing and restorative. But don't neglect your social relationships. Having a strong social network of sober friends and acquaintances can lower your stress level, improve your self-esteem, and help you stick to your recovery program. People who are socially engaged also tend to be healthier and to live longer. It's best to develop both kinds of skills—the ability to amuse yourself when alone and the ability to engage in meaningful relationships with others. So even if you're perfectly comfortable being alone, actively seek out sober friends and join social or recreational groups. And if you're uncomfortable being alone, try doing something solitary for fifteen minutes a day. You may find that you like it!

Initially, interacting with sober people may be difficult because you probably used alcohol or drugs as a protective blanket to insulate yourself from the outside world. You may have socialized with others while drinking or using, but your brain and personality were "offline," and you were not truly engaged. Your uncomfortable feelings were blotted out, or at least numbed by the drugs or alcohol. And there was no need to master the art of conversation or learn the nuances of successful social interaction as long as you were drunk or high. You'll undoubtedly feel awkward and nervous when socializing sober, but like any other set of skills, it gets easier with practice.

One of the best ways to practice is by interacting with the members of your AA or NA group, or a similar group. Like you, these people will be learning how to establish normal relationships with sober people and face their social fears while retaining their sobriety. They will know exactly how you feel (they're feeling the same way!) and can offer you a nonjudgmental, supportive social network.

> *Back to Jacob, the retired teacher mentioned earlier in the chapter who had just started to work on his alcoholism: As a part of his treatment, Jacob began to see a psychotherapist, who helped him target his unhappiness and frustration with life as a major trigger for his drinking. They worked together to compile a list of pleasurable activities for Jacob that did not involve drinking. He chose some activities that he could do alone (Sudoku, weightlifting, and stamp collecting), as well as some that he could do with friends and family (golfing, playing cards, and building a new patio cover). After making this list, Jacob realized that he had stopped doing anything fun, other than drinking, years earlier. He asked his brother to help him design and build a new patio cover for his house and found he really enjoyed the time they spent together. Jacob discovered that just by adding three or four pleasurable activities to his routine each week, his life became much fuller and more enjoyable. "Okay, doc, you win," he told me recently. "You can have fun even when you're not drinking. And I feel a lot more energetic now that I'm off the sauce."*

Learning to Think of Happiness

If the idea of interacting with sober people distresses you, remember that most of your anxiety is coming from inaccurate, negative thoughts. Under the stress of recovery, you may find it easy to believe that you'll never feel good about yourself around others and that interacting with sober folks is unfulfilling, if not downright impossible. Be sure to examine your thoughts before accepting them as the truth.

For practice, take a look at the following inaccurate, pro-addiction thoughts and put a check mark next to any statement that you agree with.

Inaccurate, Pro-Addiction Thoughts Checklist

_____ Being with sober people is scary.

_____ They won't accept me when they find out I'm an addict.

_____ My family won't ever really love me again, no matter how long I've been sober.

_____ There's no way I can ever have fun without alcohol or drugs.

_____ I don't know how to converse about anything when I'm straight; sober folks will think I'm boring.

_____ I don't want to take on a new activity, because I don't want to feel stupid while learning it.

_____ After all of the crummy things I did while drinking or using, I don't deserve to be happy.

_____ What's the point of trying to be happy? I'll relapse soon, and then it won't matter.

_____ Sober people are boring!

_____ Sobriety is serious work with no real enjoyment to be had.

_____ It's going to take me years to learn how to enjoy living without alcohol or drugs, and by then I'll be too old to have any fun.

_____ "Learn" to have fun? Who has time for that?

_____ Drinking or using may not be the smartest thing to do, but at least I always had plenty of fun and plenty of friends.

_____ How can some tight-ass counselor teach me anything about having fun?

_____ I felt a lot better about myself when I was drinking or using.

If you checked three or more of these, you are in caught in the grip of pro-addiction, irrational thinking. Reread the discussion in Chapter Two about replacing pro-addiction thoughts with pro-recovery ones, then review the examples below.

Replacing Pro-Addiction Thoughts with Pro-Recovery Thoughts

Pro-addiction thought—"Being with sober people is scary."

Pro-recovery thought—"I'll be anxious while learning to socialize in the sober world, but I know I can do it if I take it step by step. I can start with the members of my AA group, who are just like me, and also with loving family members who won't ridicule or ignore me. When I feel comfortable with them, I'll try interacting with others. There's lots to gain and no need to rush."

Pro-addiction thought—"They won't accept me when they find out I'm an addict."

Pro-recovery thought—"A lot of people won't know a thing about my past. Of those that do, a lot will only be concerned with who and what I am now. Most people have done dumb things in the past and many will respect the fact that I'm in treatment and working hard to improve myself."

Pro-addiction thought—"My family won't ever really love me again, no matter how long I've been sober."

Pro-recovery thought—"It's true that some family members are angry at me, which is reasonable given my past behavior. But it's also true that they love me and want nothing more than for me to stay sober and have a productive and enjoyable life. It will take a while for the resentment to heal, but by sticking to my recovery program, I'll be able to regain their respect and good will."

Pro-addiction thought—"There's no way I can ever have fun without alcohol or drugs.

Pro-recovery thought—"I *can* have fun without alcohol or drugs. My brother is a lot of fun, and he never touches alcohol. Maybe I should give him a call."

Now try rewriting the following pro-addiction thoughts to make them pro-recovery thoughts:

Pro-Recovery Thoughts Worksheet

Pro-addiction thought—After all of the crummy things I did while drinking or using, I don't deserve to be happy.

Pro-recovery thought— _____

_____

Pro-addiction thought—What's the point of trying to be happy? I'll relapse soon, and then it won't matter.

Pro-recovery thought— _____

_____

Pro-addiction thought—Sober people are boring!

Pro-recovery thought— _____

_____

Pro-addiction thought—Sobriety is serious work with no real enjoyment to be had.

Pro-recovery thought— _____

_____

Pro-addiction thought—It's going to take me years to learn how to enjoy living without alcohol or drugs, and by then I'll be too old to have any fun.

Pro-recovery thought— _____

_____

> *Pro-addiction thought*—Drinking or using may not be the smartest thing to do, but at least I always had plenty of fun and plenty of friends.
>
> *Pro-recovery thought*— _____
>
> _____

Whenever inaccurate negative thinking threatens to disrupt your happiness or sobriety, replace those thoughts with pro-recovery thoughts. This is perhaps the most effective way to keep yourself on the road to a productive and enjoyable sober life.

Helping Yourself by Helping Others

Scientists generally agree that humans are social animals designed to work with each other and that, on a very basic level, we really enjoy helping others. Perhaps one day we'll find out that there's a special code in our DNA that makes us feel good about helping each other. Until then, we can point to thousands of years of human experience that lend credence to the idea that one of the best ways to feel good about yourself is to do something for someone else.

What you do for others doesn't have to cost you a lot of money or take a lot of time. In fact, sometimes the simplest things are best. For example, you can:

- Call someone just to ask, "How are you feeling today?"
- Send a card saying, "I'm thinking of you."
- Pay a genuine compliment: "You look nice in that dress."
- Say a prayer for someone else: "Dear God, please look after my friend."
- Give a hug to someone who needs one.
- Tell a joke to someone who could use a lift.

- Stop by just to say hello.

- When you're going to the store, see if you can pick up something for someone who doesn't get out much.

- Give someone a pat on the back for a job well done.

- Say "thank you" for the five minutes of attention someone gave you.

- Think of someone who cared about you but was hurt by your actions, then do something nice for them.

- Donate money to charity.

It doesn't take much to make someone smile. And it doesn't take much in the way of giving to make you feel very good about yourself. Even if you haven't yet discovered what your enjoyable activities may be, or you're still uncomfortable interacting with sober people, you can increase your happiness quotient by doing something for someone else.

Some Ways to Brighten Your Own Day

Happiness and good cheer begin with you. Here are a few examples of ways you can find a sense of accomplishment or bring a smile to your lips—or both!

1. Have a winter picnic. Invite some friends, put a blanket down on the floor, and serve pizza or fried chicken, potato salad, and coleslaw. If you are ambitious, you can even wheel out the barbecue and make some burgers! Use paper plates so there are no dishes to do later.

2. Go out to the garage, pull out your tools, and start working on that bookshelf or other item you've been thinking of building for years.

3. Rent a movie that takes place in a tropical setting, and imagine yourself relaxing on the beach.

4. Get out your old baseball mitt and bat, call up a (sober) buddy, meet him at the park, and have some fun tossing and hitting the ball around.

5. Clean out your closet, and donate to charity everything that no longer fits or is out of style. (You'll be helping others while organizing yourself—that should be worth two smiles!)

6. Remember those action-adventure movies you loved as a kid and teenager? Grab a (sober) buddy and head to the theater for an afternoon of popcorn and fun.

7. Try something new. Take a cooking, dance, or martial arts class.

8. Do something outside in the snow. Go skating or sledding, build a snowman, have a snowball fight, or take a walk in a park.

9. Go to the zoo, laugh at the antics of the monkeys, admire the beauty of the antelope, marvel at the strength of the lions.

10. Turn off the TV—instead of aimlessly flipping channels, read a book, play a board game, or work on a jigsaw puzzle. You'll be surprised how much fun it can be to engage your mind!

11. Eat an ice cream sundae with all of your favorite toppings. Or have a sundae party, with each guest assigned to bring one topping.

12. Make a fancy meal for your family. Find new recipes, and expand your skills.

13. Get a massage, facial, manicure, or pedicure. (This is for guys, too!) Schedule it a week in advance so that you have something to look forward to.

14. Say no to something you really can't or shouldn't do. (This is not an excuse to avoid doing your chores!)

15. Put a "Do Not Disturb" sign on the bathroom door, and take a bubble bath. Don't forget the music and candles.

16. Wake up your inner child, and paint a picture with finger paint. Remember to display your artwork on the refrigerator.

17. Watch a sitcom, comedy movie, or cartoon, and laugh out loud.

18. Take some uninterrupted time for yourself. Don't answer your phone for a full day. Let the messages go to voice mail, and return calls later, if necessary.

Whatever you do, don't just sit there. Once you get out and do something, the blahs will usually disappear.

You've Gotta Want It

Once upon a time, your substance of choice was your main source of pleasure and the focal point of your socializing. Now that's no longer the case. That's great! But it's also a challenge, because you must learn to find the joy in life without the "help" of a substance. It's especially difficult if your brain has sustained damage due to the substance use. You may feel awash in depression and anxiety, fearing that recovery is impossible. These are normal feelings that can and will fade away with time, if you maintain your sobriety. If you're patient and persistent, you will find that it's entirely possible to find joy in sober life, the kind of joy that is simply unavailable to those in active addiction.

There's no great secret to happiness, no magical list of things to do. Keep looking for reasons to smile, and eventually your smiles will start to happen on their own. You'll learn to derive pleasure and satisfaction in the everyday-ness of your life. If you truly desire joy and happiness, you're halfway there already.

Key Points Review

- We all want to be happy, but some of us have forgotten what true happiness is. One thing is certain: Happiness is *not* simply the absence of pain.

- It can be difficult to be happy during recovery, as you can no longer rely on alcohol or drugs to help you "have fun" and ease the ordinary and extraordinary stresses of life.

- Having (sober) fun is an acquired skill that may take planning, practice, and persistence.

- Fortunately there are hundreds of fun activities, ranging from archery to hiking, from talking with friends to going to the beach to engaging in hobbies.

- Interacting with sober friends can be a great source of happiness. Don't be deterred because you haven't socialized with sober people in a long time. With practice, you'll soon be comfortable with sober people again.

- You can practice sober socializing in AA or other 12-step groups.

- If you find yourself thinking that there's no such thing as sober happiness, or that sober people won't accept you, replace those pro-addiction thoughts with pro-recovery thoughts.

- You can increase your happiness by helping others. Simply telling a joke to someone who needs a lift can make you happier.

- There is no secret to happiness. If you want to be happy, seek out pleasurable activities and people and stick with your quest for happiness through the uncomfortable times. You *can* learn to be happy again.

CHAPTER TWELVE

True Recovery— Maintaining Your Goals for Life

The road to recovery for the alcoholic or addict is a long one, and it can sometimes seem endless. Patients and families have often told me that they simply cannot see the light shining at the end of the tunnel. This is understandable, especially when you realize that no one is ever completely "cured" of addiction; it's a lifelong disease that must be managed each and every day. But as I often remind my patients and their families and friends, every day without drinking or using is a bright and glorious day. Every little step forward is a tremendous milestone. And, thanks to our new treatment paradigm, the odds of recovery are better than ever before that you'll achieve true recovery.

Our new understanding of addiction is that it is a chronic illness that attacks and damages the brain. This idea sweeps away two myths that have hampered addiction treatment for decades: that addiction is a kind of "personality disease," and that "talking therapy" is its only significant treatment. The old way of treating addiction has an abysmally low success rate of only 20–30 percent, while the new way increases the rate to levels approaching 90 percent. That's because the new anti-addiction medicines can help repair addiction-related brain damage and greatly enhance one's ability to focus on and benefit from therapy and 12-step programs. Once the major roadblocks of cravings, brain damage, depression, anxiety, and other mental and emotional problems are out of the way (or at least under control), the addicted person is in a much better position to absorb and apply the psychological concepts that can transform his or her life.

Vivitrol and Suboxone both reduce cravings and make it almost impossible to get high from alcohol, heroin, and prescription opiates. Campral speeds repairs to the damaged brain, allowing it to understand and adopt new ways of thinking and living. Other medicines reduce the depression, anxiety, mania, psychosis, and other mental ailments that often interfere with the recovery process. These medicines are essential, as they make it possible for the addict to concentrate on and benefit from a treatment program. Of course, talking therapies are still essential to the recovery process, as are mastering new coping skills and making permanent lifestyle modifications. But with cravings under control and the brain better able to focus and understand, it becomes markedly easier to master the skills necessary to live a sober, productive, and happy life.

To supplement your learning, the information found on www.Enter Health.com/HealingtheAddictedBrain can help you delve deeper into the ideas and tools that have been introduced in this book. The easy availability of such resources means you can continue to reeducate yourself and everyone in your support system throughout your life. It allows you to refine and maintain your goals that you set early on in your new sobriety, so that you can evolve and adapt successfully to new stresses as they confront you along the way.

With a new paradigm and new medicines, coupled with online programs offering psychological and practical strategies to manage addiction, the future looks brighter than ever. I am confident that you can leave your alcohol and drug addictions behind and take your rightful place in the world as a happy, healthy, and sober individual. It's a brand new day— make it the beginning of a brand new life!

Acknowledgments

Sincere thanks to Barry Fox for his invaluable assistance in transforming my critical concepts into stimulating and engaging text easily understood by all. Also, I would like to acknowledge the significant contribution of time and passion by Dr. Joyce Scallan, who helped me to organize and present my original content in a coherent fashion.

Index

About the Author

Harold C. Urschel III, MD, attended Princeton University, graduating cum laude with a bachelor of arts in neuropsychology. He obtained his doctorate of medicine from the University of Texas Southwestern Medical School. After completing the first three years of his psychiatric residency at UT Southwestern and Parkland Memorial Hospital in Dallas, Dr. Urschel moved to Philadelphia to finish his residency and begin a two-year chemical dependency treatment clinical research fellowship at the University of Pennsylvania/Veteran's Administration Medical Center. Dr. Urschel also earned a masters of management administration degree from Stanford University Graduate School of Business. He is currently board certified in addiction and general psychiatry by the American Board of Medical Specialties.

As co-founder and chief medical strategist of EnterHealth, LLC, Dr. Urschel is responsible for overseeing and implementing all addiction psychiatric treatments delivered through traditional clinical outlets, telemedicine support, and online coaching services (www.EnterHealth.com/HealingtheAddictedBrain). He is also the founder and CEO of the Dallas-based Urschel Recovery Science Institute, whose mission is to provide the best outpatient, science-based addiction treatment services available in a discreet, professional, and highly personalized manner (www.recovery-science.com). His Recovery Science program has also been adopted as the clinical addiction treatment program for the University of Texas Southwestern Medical School's Department of Psychiatry in the past.

A principal investigator in clinical research trials, Dr. Urschel also founded CNS Research Group, LLP, which provides research services for clinical trials in addiction and general psychiatry. He has personally participated in numerous major multi-site trials in the areas of general psychiatric research as well as advanced psychopharmacological research on medications targeted at addiction recovery.